P O C K E T

SPACE FACTS

Written by
CAROLE STOTT and
CLINT TWIST

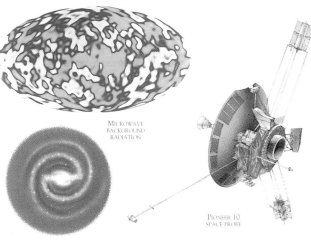

MICROWAVE
BACKGROUND
RADIATION

PIONEER 10
SPACE PROBE

BARRED SPIRAL GALAXY

DK PUBLISHING

LONDON, NEW YORK,
MELBOURNE, MUNICH, and DELHI

Project editor Clint Twist
Art editor Alexandra Brown
Senior editor Laura Buller
Senior art editor Helen Senior
Editorial consultant Carole Stott
Picture research Fiona Watson
Production Louise Barratt
US editor Jill Hamilton
US consultant Dr. William A. Gutsch

REVISED EDITION
Project editor Steve Setford
Designer Sarah Crouch
Managing editor Linda Esposito
Managing art editor Jane Thomas
DTP designer Siu Yin Ho
Consultant Ian Ridpath
Production Erica Rosen
US editors Margaret Parrish, Christine Heilman

This book is dedicated to the memory of Janet MacLennan

Second American Edition, 2003
Published in the United States by
DK Publishing, Inc., 375 Hudson Street,
New York, New York 10014

03 04 05 06 07 08 10 9 8 7 6 5 4 3 2 1

A Cataloging-in-Publication record for the First American Edition of this book
is available from the Library of Congress.

ISBN 0-7894-9593-7

Color reproduction by Colourscan, Singapore
Printed and bound in Italy by L.E.G.O.

See our complete product line at
www.dk.com

CONTENTS

HOW TO USE THIS BOOK

These pages show you how to use *Pockets: Space Facts*.
The book is divided into nine sections. Each section
contains information on one aspect of space or space
exploration. At the beginning of each section there
is a picture page and a guide to the contents of
that section.

*Corner
coding*

OBJECTS IN SPACE
Some of the sections deal with
objects in space, such as galaxies,
stars, and planets. Other sections
deal with the appearance of these
objects in Earth's sky.

Heading →

CORNER CODING
The page corners
are color coded
according to
the section.

■ UNIVERSE

■ GALAXIES

□ STARS

■ SPACE FROM EARTH

■ SOLAR SYSTEM

■ PLANETS

■ SMALL OBJECTS

■ STUDYING SPACE

■ SPACE HISTORY

Introduction →

HEADING
This describes the
subject of the page.
This page is about
Saturn. If a subject
continues over
several pages, the
same heading applies.

Data box →

DATA BOXES
Some pages have data
boxes. These contain
detailed numerical
information, such as
the distances between
galaxies, stars, planets,
and moons. This data is
often set out in tables.

SATURN
FAMED FOR ITS magnificent
ring system, Saturn is the
second largest of the planets.
Like its nearest neighbor
Jupiter, Saturn is a gas
giant. However, the mass
is so spread out that on
average the planet is less
dense than water. Titan is
the largest of Saturn's 30
moons. It has a very thick
atmosphere and is bigger
than the planet Mercury.

SATURN PLANET FACTS	
Average distance from the Sun	886.7 million miles (1,427 million km)
Orbital period	29.45 Earth years
Orbital velocity	6 miles (9.7 km/sec)
Rotation period	10.23 hours
Diameter at equator	74,897 miles (120,536 km)
Cloud-top temperature	-292°F (-180°C)
Mass (Earth = 1)	95
Gravity (Earth = 1)	0.92
Number of moons	30

SATURN FACTS
• Saturn's rings are
less than 1.2 miles
(2 km) thick, but over
50 miles (750,000 km)
in diameter.
• The rings consist
of billions of ice-
covered rock
fragments and
dust particles.

Fact box

FACT BOXES
Many pages have fact boxes.
These contain at-a-glance
information about the subject,
such as the temperature at the
core of a typical star, or the
brightest planet in Earth's sky.

8

INTRODUCTION

This provides you with a summary and overview of the subject. After reading the introduction, you should have a clear idea of what the following page, or pages, are about.

RUNNING HEADS

These remind you which section you are in. The top of the left-hand page gives the section name. The right-hand page gives the section. This page on Saturn is from the planets section.

CAPTIONS AND ANNOTATIONS

Most illustrations have an explanatory caption. Annotations, in *italics*, draw your attention to particular features of an illustration and usually have leader lines.

Caption

Running head

Label

Annotation

LABELS

For extra clarity, some pictures have labels. The labels may identify a picture when it is not obvious from the text what it is, or they may give extra information about the subject.

NUMBERS

Large numbers are often given in standard scientific notation – as a number with just one digit left of the decimal point multiplied by a power of ten. For example, $1.8 \times 10^8 =$
$1.8 \times 10 \times 10 \times 10 \times 10 \times 10 \times 10 \times 10 \times 10$.

GREEK ALPHABET

Greek letters are used to identify stars.

α	alpha	ν	nu
β	beta	ξ	xi
γ	gamma	o	omicron
δ	delta	π	pi
ϵ	epsilon	ρ	rho
ζ	zeta	σ	sigma
η	eta	τ	tau
θ	theta	υ	upsilon
ι	iota	ϕ	phi
κ	kappa	χ	chi
λ	lambda	ψ	psi

INDEX AND GLOSSARY

There is a subject index at the back of the book which alphabetically lists every subject. There is also an alphabetical glossary that explains the meaning of the scientific and technical terms used in this book.

UNIVERSE

WHAT IS THE UNIVERSE?

THE UNIVERSE IS EVERYTHING that exists. From the Earth beneath our feet to the farthest stars, everything is a part of the universe. The universe is so large that it contains countless billions of stars. However, most of it consists of nothing but empty space.

Galaxies

Galaxy containing billions of stars

Quasar – the brilliant center of a distant galaxy

Supernova – the death of a large star

Comet – a dirty snowball

LOOKING TO THE SKIES

From Earth, we can look into space and study the universe. In every direction we look there are stars. There are more stars in the universe than any other type of object – stars at different stages of their lives in enormous groups called galaxies, including at least one star that has planets. Despite the huge size of the universe, we know of only one place where life exists – planet Earth.

UNIVERSE FACTS

• There are at least a trillion galaxies in the universe; large ones contain more than a trillion stars.

• The most distant objects we can detect are 87,000 million million million miles (139,000 million million million km) away.

HORSEHEAD IN SPACE
Looking like a chess knight, the Horsehead Nebula (right) is a gigantic cloud of dark-colored dust. It is visible because the dust blocks out light from behind the nebula, so that we see it in silhouette. The universe contains many similar clouds that block our view of different regions.

Pulsar – a rapidly rotating neutron star

The Sun – an ordinary middle-aged star

Cluster of stars

Planets – balls of rock, ice, or gas

Nebula – a cloud of gas and dust

VISUALIZING THE UNIVERSE
The easiest way to think of the universe is as a sphere which is constantly expanding so that everything is getting farther away from everything else. There is nothing beyond the universe, because the universe contains all of time and space within it.

SCALE OF THE UNIVERSE

DISTANCES IN THE UNIVERSE are so great that the light-year is used as a unit of measurement. Light travels at about 186,000 miles/sec (300,000 km/s), and a light-year (ly) is the distance light travels in one year. A galaxy can measure thousands of light-years across and be millions of light-years distant.

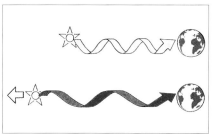

LIGHT AND MOTION
A star's light can tell us about its motion. If the star is moving away from Earth, its light is stretched by comparison with stationary stars. Light from a star moving away is also shifted toward the red end of the spectrum. Stars approaching Earth have compressed light shifted toward blue.

SCALE OF SIZES
The human world, the world of everyday experience, is dwarfed by the scale of the universe. Earth is one of nine planets orbiting the Sun, which is one of about 200 billion stars in the Milky Way galaxy.

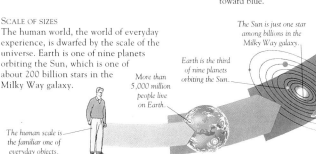

The Sun is just one star among billions in the Milky Way galaxy.

Earth is the third of nine planets orbiting the Sun.

More than 5,000 million people live on Earth.

The human scale is the familiar one of everyday objects.

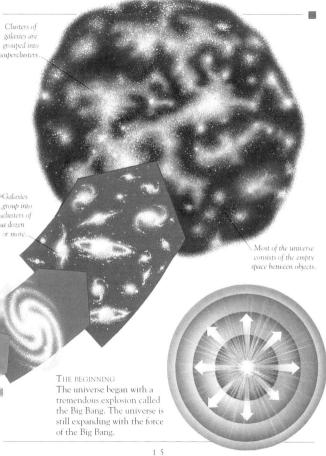

Clusters of galaxies are grouped into superclusters.

Galaxies group into clusters of a dozen or more.

Most of the universe consists of the empty space between objects.

THE BEGINNING
The universe began with a tremendous explosion called the Big Bang. The universe is still expanding with the force of the Big Bang.

1 5

LIFE STORY OF THE UNIVERSE

ALL MATTER, ENERGY, space, and time were created in the Big Bang around 14 billion years ago. At first the universe was small and very hot. As the universe expanded and cooled, atomic particles joined to form hydrogen and helium. Over billions of years these gases have produced galaxies, stars, planets, and us.

The Big Bang creates the universe

Universe keeps expanding

The universe will slowly cool as it gets ever larger and less dense.

WHAT HAPPENS NEXT?

The universe has been expanding since the Big Bang, and will probably go on expanding for ever. Recent observations indicate that the expansion is speeding up as the universe gets older and bigger.

BIG BANG RIPPLES

This map of the whole sky is based on tiny variations in the temperature of space. Red is warmer than average and blue is colder. These tiny variations are irregularities of the Big Bang explosion. The information for the map was obtained by the Cosmic Background Explorer Satellite (COBE).

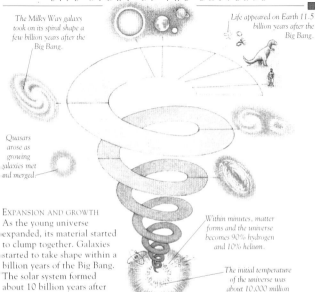

The Milky Way galaxy took on its spiral shape a few billion years after the Big Bang.

Life appeared on Earth 11.5 billion years after the Big Bang.

Quasars arose as growing galaxies met and merged.

EXPANSION AND GROWTH
As the young universe expanded, its material started to clump together. Galaxies started to take shape within a billion years of the Big Bang. The solar system formed about 10 billion years after the Big Bang.

Within minutes, matter forms and the universe becomes 90% hydrogen and 10% helium.

The initial temperature of the universe was about 10,000 million million million degrees

UNIVERSE: COOLING DATA	
Time after Big Bang	Temperature
10^{-6} secs	$1.8 \times 10^{13}°F$ ($10^{13}°C$)
3 minutes	$1.8 \times 10^{9}°F$ ($10^{9}°C$)
300,000 years	18,000°F (10,000°C)
1 million years	5,400°F (3,000°C)
1,000 million years	−275°F (−170°C)
15,000 million years	−454°F (−270°C)

UNIVERSE FACT
• Scientists can trace the life story of the universe back to what is called the Planck time, 10^{-43} seconds after the Big Bang. 10^{-43} means a decimal point followed by 42 zeros and then a one.

GALAXIES

WHAT IS A GALAXY?

A GALAXY IS an enormous group of stars. A large galaxy may have a billion, a small galaxy only a few hundred thousand. Even small galaxies are so big that it takes light thousands of years to cross them. Galaxies are formed from vast spinning clouds of gas. Many continue to spin. Galaxies come in a number of different shapes.

DISTANT STAR CITY
The Andromeda galaxy is so far away that its light takes 2,500,000 years to travel to Earth. We see the galaxy as it was 2,500,000 years ago.

GALAXIES: THE FOUR
BASIC TYPES

ELLIPTICAL
These range from ball-shaped to egg-shaped. They contain mainly old stars, and are the most common type.

SPIRAL
These are disk-shaped. Most material is in the spiral arms where new stars are formed. Old stars are in the nucleus.

BARRED-SPIRAL
These are like spiral galaxies, but the nucl is elongated into a ba The spiral arms exten from the ends of the l

BRIGHTEST LIGHTS
This is an X-ray image of a
quasi-stellar object, one of
the brightest, and remotest
objects. The most distant
are about 15 billion light-
years away. Known as
quasars, they are probably
the cores of the first
galaxies to be formed.

BRIGHT GALAXIES: DATA		
Galaxy	Distance	Type
Andromeda (M31)	2,500,000 ly	Sb
M33	2,800,000 ly	Sc
NGC 300	4,200,000 ly	Sc
NGC 55	5,800,000 ly	Sc
NGC 253	8,000,000 ly	Sc
M81	14,000,000 ly	Sb
M82	14,000,000 ly	peculiar
Centaurus A	16,000,000 ly	E (peculiar)
M83	16,000,000 ly	SBc
M101	17,000,000 ly	Sc
M64	18,000,000 ly	Sab
Whirlpool (M51)	27,000,000 ly	Sbc
M104	44,000,000 ly	Sa/b
M87	55,000,000 ly	E0
M100	55,000,000 ly	Sc
M77	62,000,000 ly	Sb
NGC 1316 (Fornax A)	66,000,000 ly	Sa (peculiar)

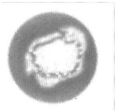

IRREGULAR
Some of these have a
hint of spiral structure,
while others do not fit
any known pattern.
They are the rarest type.

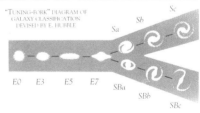

"TUNING-FORK" DIAGRAM OF
GALAXY CLASSIFICATION
DEVISED BY E. HUBBLE

Sc

Sb

Sa

E0   E3   E5   E7

SBa

SBb

SBc

CLASSIFYING GALAXIES BY SHAPE
Elliptical galaxies are classified from E0 (spherical)
to E7 (very flattened). Spirals (S) and barred spirals
(SB) are graded from a to c, according to the
compactness of the central nucleus and the tightness
of the arms. Irregular galaxies (Irr) are not shown
here, but can be divided into types I and II.

CLUSTERS AND SUPERCLUSTERS

GALAXIES OCCUR TOGETHER in clusters that range in size from a few to a few thousand galaxies. Clusters themselves also occur in groups called superclusters, which are the largest structures in the universe.

NEIGHBORING CLUSTER
The Virgo cluster is about 55 million light-years away, but it is the nearest major cluster to our own Local Group.

Milky Way

M31

M33

THE LOCAL GROUP
Our own cluster is about five million light-years across and contains about 36 galaxies. The largest galaxies in the Local Group are Andromeda (M31), Triangulum (M33), and our own Milky Way galaxy.

SUPERCLUSTER FACTS

• The average distance between galaxies in a cluster is about ten galaxy diameters.

• The Local Group is just one small part of a giant supercluster about 100 million light-years in diameter.

SOME LOCAL GROUP GALAXIES: DATA

Name	Diameter	Distance
Andromeda	150,000 ly	2,500,000 ly
M33	40,000 ly	2,800,000 ly
Large Magellanic Cloud (LMC)	30,000 ly	170,000 ly
Small Magellanic Cloud (SMC)	20,000 ly	190,000 ly
NGC 6822	15,000 ly	1,650,000 ly
NGC 205	11,000 ly	2,700,000 ly

HONEYCOMB SPACE

Superclusters tend to be flattened into disks or sheets, or elongated into filaments. These shapes cannot be seen through a telescope, but scientists now know that the large-scale structure of the universe is basically a honeycomb arrangement. Superclusters are arranged on the surface of immense "bubbles." These bubbles are almost completely empty of matter. They are huge voids that contain only a few atoms of gas.

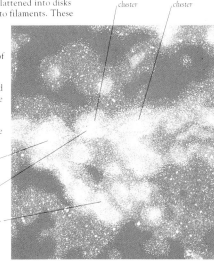

Coma cluster

Ursa Major cluster

Local Group

Virgo cluster

Leo cloud

THE LOCAL
SUPERCLUSTER

THE MILKY WAY

THE SUN IS JUST ONE of the more than 100 billion stars in our own galaxy – the Milky Way. Ours is a spiral galaxy, with a nucleus of old stars surrounded by a halo of even older stars. All the young stars are located in the spiral arms. The Milky Way is so large that it takes light 100,000 years to travel from edge to edge. All the stars we see at night are in the Milky Way.

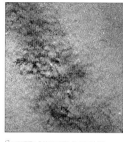

SAGITTARIUS STAR CLOUD
This infrared image shows young stars in Sagittarius, looking toward the Milky Way's center. Infrared reveals millions of stars that are obscured by dust clouds when viewed in visible light.

From the side the spiral arms look like a flattened disk

Galactic halo contains the oldest stars

MILKY WAY GALAXY:
EXTERNAL SIDE VIEW

Nucleus is the brightest region of the galaxy

SIDE-ON SPIRAL
Viewed from the side, from a distance of about a million light-years, the Milky Way galaxy would look like a giant lens – with flattened edges and a bright central nucleus. Around the nucleus is a roughly spherical halo that contains the oldest stars in the galaxy.

MILKY WAY FACTS
• The Milky Way is now thought to be a barred spiral galaxy.
• Our galaxy rotates. The Sun takes about 220 million years to make one revolution – a period sometimes known as a "cosmic year." Stars in other parts of the galaxy travel at different rates.

ABOVE THE SPIRAL

From above, or below, the spiral arms of the Milky Way galaxy would be clearly visible. These contain most of the galaxy's gas and dust, and this is where star-forming regions are found.

THE MILKY WAY AS SEEN FROM EARTH

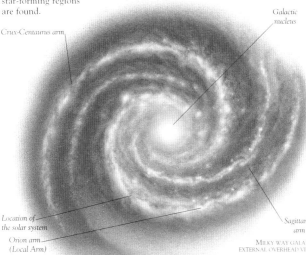

Crux-Centaurus arm

Galactic nucleus

Location of the solar system

Orion arm (Local Arm)

Sagittarius arm

MILKY WAY GALAXY: EXTERNAL OVERHEAD VIEW

THE LOCAL ARM

THE SOLAR SYSTEM is situated about two-thirds of the way from the galaxy's center, at the edge of a spiral arm called the Local Arm or the Orion Arm. From this viewpoint, we see the galaxy as a great milky river of stars across the night sky.

The galactic nucleus is more than 15,000 ly across.

POSITION OF THE
LOCAL ARM IN
THE GALAXY

SEVEN STARRY SISTERS
The Pleiades is a cluster of bright stars, seven of which can be seen with the naked eye, hence their popular name – the Seven Sisters – which has been in use for at least 2,000 years. In fact there are more than 200 stars in the cluster, which formed about 60 million years ago – shortly after the dinosaurs died out on Earth.

SPECTACULAR END

The Dumbbell Nebula, located about 1,000 light-years from the Sun, is a single star nearing the end of its life. Spherical shells of gas are blown out from the star's surface, making a spectacular sight. Gradually the gas will disperse, and will eventually be used to form new stars elsewhere in the galaxy.

LOCAL ARM FACTS

• From edge to edge the Dumbbell Nebula is two light-years in diameter.

• Some stars in Taurus and Orion are less than 1 million years old – mere star babies compared with our own Sun, which is 5 billion years old.

• The nearest bright star cluster to the Sun is the Hyades about 150 light-years away. The Hyades forms the V-shape of the bull's head in the constellation of Taurus.

THE LOCAL REGION OF SPACE WITHIN 1,000 LIGHT-YEARS OF THE SUN

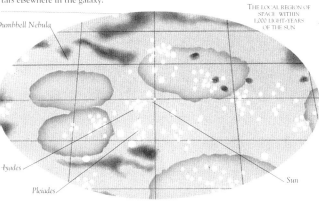

Dumbbell Nebula

Hyades

Pleiades

Sun

STARS

WHAT IS A STAR?

A STAR IS an enormous spinning ball of hot and luminous gas. Most stars contain two main gases – hydrogen and helium. These gases are held together by gravity, and at the core they are very densely packed. Within the core, immense amounts of energy are produced.

STAR CLUSTER
The cluster M13 in the constellation of Hercules contains hundreds of thousands of stars arranged in a compact ball.

Temperature and pressure increase toward the core.

STRUCTURE OF A STAR

Energy is released at the surface as light and heat.

Energy is produced by nuclear reactions in the core.

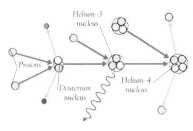

Helium-3 nucleus

Protons

Deuterium nucleus

Helium-4 nucleus

CORE FUSION

A star produces energy by nuclear fusion. Within the core, hydrogen nuclei (protons) collide and fuse to form first deuterium (heavy hydrogen) and then two forms of helium. During fusion, energy is given off. This type of reaction, which is found in most stars, is called the proton-proton chain.

VARYING SIZES

Stars differ greatly in the amount of gas they contain, and in their size. The largest stars are 1,000 times the diameter of the Sun, while the smallest are just a fraction of its size – not much bigger than the planet Jupiter.

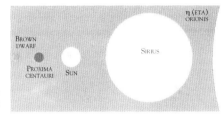

η (ETA) ORIONIS

BROWN DWARF

PROXIMA CENTAURI

SUN

SIRIUS

PROMINENT STARS: DATA		
Name	Designation	Distance
Vega	α Lyrae	25 ly
Pollux	β Geminorum	34 ly
Capella	α Aurigae	42 ly
Aldebaran	α Tauri	65 ly
Regulus	α Leonis	77 ly
Spica	α Virginis	262 ly
Canopus	α Carinae	313 ly
Betelgeuse	α Orionis	427 ly
Polaris	α Ursae Minoris	431 ly

STAR FACTS

• All the chemical elements heavier than hydrogen, helium, and lithium were made by nuclear reactions inside stars.

• The mass of the Sun – 1 solar mass – is used as a standard for measuring other stars.

STAR BIRTH

STARS FOLLOW a life cycle that lasts millions to billions of years. All stars begin in the same way as material in a nebula, a cloud of gas and dust. Stars are not born individually, but in groups called clusters. Initially, the stars in a cluster have roughly the same composition. Despite these early similarities, the stars usually develop at different rates, and most clusters drift apart before very long.

STELLAR BIRTHPLACE
In the Orion Nebula light from new stars illuminates the dust clouds. The stars themselves remain hidden by the dust. One of these young stars is 10,000 times brighter than the Sun.

FORMATION AND EARLY DEVELOPMENT OF A STAR

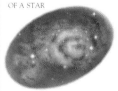

Inside a nebula, gravity causes spinning balls of gas to form – these are known as protostars.

The protostar (seen here in cross-section) shrinks, and its core becomes denser. An outer halo of gas and dust develops.

When the core reaches critical density, nuclear reactions start. The energy released blows away most of the halo.

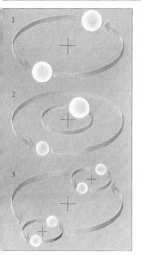

SINGLE OR DOUBLE

The Sun is unusual – it is a solitary star. Most stars come in pairs or even larger families. Multiple stars may orbit around a common center of gravity (diagrams 1 and 2, left), and may also orbit around one another (3). Double stars often appear to be variable in their light output (below) because one star regularly blocks the light of the other.

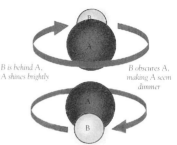

B is behind A,
A shines brightly

B obscures A,
making A seem
dimmer

As the young star continues to spin rapidly, the remaining gas and dust become flattened into a disk.

In some cases, such as around the star we call the Sun, this disk of gas and dust has formed into a system of orbiting planets.

With or without planets, the new star now shines steadily, converting hydrogen to helium by nuclear fusion.

LIFE CYCLE OF A STAR

A STAR'S LIFE CYCLE depends on its mass. Stars of the same mass as the Sun shine steadily for about 10 billion years. More massive stars convert their hydrogen more quickly, and have shorter lives. The Sun is halfway through its life. In about 5 billion years, it will expand to become a red giant star, and then collapse and end as a dwarf star.

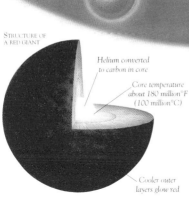

Star converting hydrogen i.e. in the main sequence

STRUCTURE OF A RED GIANT

Helium converted to carbon in core

Core temperature about 180 million°F (100 million°C)

Cooler outer layers glow red

RED GIANTS

When most of the hydrogen has been converted to helium, the star becomes a red giant – converting helium to carbon. The core heats up causing the surface to expand and cool. A red giant may expand to more than 100 times its former size.

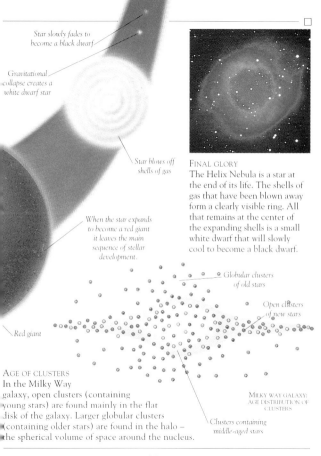

*Star slowly fades to
become a black dwarf*

*Gravitational
collapse creates a
white dwarf star*

*Star blows off
shells of gas*

*When the star expands
to become a red giant
it leaves the main
sequence of stellar
development.*

Red giant

FINAL GLORY
The Helix Nebula is a star at
the end of its life. The shells of
gas that have been blown away
form a clearly visible ring. All
that remains at the center of
the expanding shells is a small
white dwarf that will slowly
cool to become a black dwarf.

*Globular clusters
of old stars*

*Open clusters
of new stars*

AGE OF CLUSTERS
In the Milky Way
galaxy, open clusters (containing
young stars) are found mainly in the flat
disk of the galaxy. Larger globular clusters
(containing older stars) are found in the halo –
the spherical volume of space around the nucleus.

MILKY WAY GALAXY:
AGE DISTRIBUTION OF
CLUSTERS

*Clusters containing
middle-aged stars*

DEATH OF MASSIVE STARS

THE WAY A STAR DIES depends on its mass. The most
massive stars end their lives by simply exploding.
This huge explosion is called a supernova, and may
be bright enough to briefly outshine an entire galaxy.
What happens next depends
on how much stellar
material is left after
the supernova.

EXPLOSIVE COLLAPSE
Stars of at least eight
solar masses end as
supernovae. Gravity
causes them to collapse
with incredible force
producing shock waves.

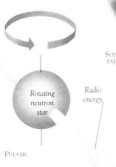

SUPERNOVA
EXPLOSION

Temperature at co
18 billion°F
(10 billion°C)

Rotating
neutron
star

Radio
energy

PULSAR

NEUTRON SPINNER
If the core that remains after a supernova is
between 1.4 and 3.0 solar masses, it forms what is
called a neutron star. Composed of super-dense
material, neutron stars spin very quickly and
produce beams of radio energy that appear to flash
on and off very rapidly. These are called pulsars.

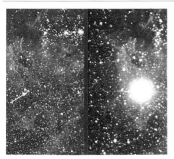

A RARE AND SPECTACULAR SIGHT

Although supernovae are fairly common in the universe, they are rarely visible to the naked eye. In 1987 a supernova was observed in the Large Magellanic Cloud, a nearby galaxy. The left-hand photograph shows the normal appearance of the star (arrowed). The supernova (designated SN 1987A) is clearly visible in the right-hand picture. After shining brightly for a few months, it slowly faded from view.

BLACK HOLES

If the core left after a supernova exceeds three solar masses, it will collapse until it becomes a black hole – something so dense that its gravity will suck in even light. By definition black holes are invisible, but they are believed to be surrounded by a spinning accretion disk of material being drawn into the black hole.

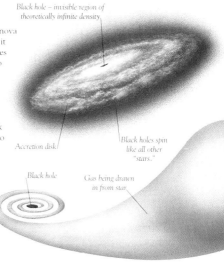

Black hole – invisible region of theoretically infinite density

Black holes spin like all other "stars."

Accretion disk

STELLAR THEFT

If a black hole forms near another star, it may suck in gas from the star, gradually stealing its mass. Astronomers believe that the object known as Cygnus X-1 is a star/black hole pair.

Black hole

Gas being drawn in from star

STELLAR CLASSIFICATION

THE MASS OF A STAR affects its other properties – its color, temperature, and luminosity. Each star is different, but by studying their properties, astronomers have been able to devise a system that enables them to classify all stars.

O		72,000°F
B		(40,000°C)
A		18,000°F
		(10,000°C)
F		13,500°F
		(7,5000°C)
G		10,800°F
		(6,000°C)
K		9,000°F
		(5,000°C)
		6,300°F
M		(3,500°C)

HEAT AND LIGHT

A star's color is usually a good indicator of its temperature. Blue stars are the hottest, and red the coolest. The Harvard system uses letters of the alphabet to classify stars according to their surface temperature. This diagram shows the color and temperature range of the main types.

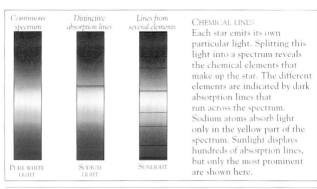

Continuous spectrum	Distinctive absorption lines	Lines from several elements
PURE WHITE LIGHT	SODIUM LIGHT	SUNLIGHT

CHEMICAL LINES

Each star emits its own particular light. Splitting this light into a spectrum reveals the chemical elements that make up the star. The different elements are indicated by dark absorption lines that run across the spectrum. Sodium atoms absorb light only in the yellow part of the spectrum. Sunlight displays hundreds of absorption lines, but only the most prominent are shown here.

HERTZSPRUNG-RUSSELL (HR) DIAGRAM OF STELLAR CLASSIFICATION

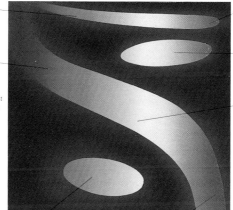

Supergiant stars e.g. Deneb

Betelgeuse is a red supergiant.

Main sequence stars, e.g. Sirius A, which convert hydrogen to helium

Arcturus is a red giant.

The Sun is a main sequence yellow dwarf.

White dwarf stars e.g. Sirius B

Barnard's Star is a main sequence red dwarf.

COLOR-CODED DIAGRAM

The HR diagram plots a star's temperature against its absolute magnitude (the amount of light it gives off). The brightest stars are at the top, and the dimmest are near the bottom. The hottest stars are to the left and the coolest to the right. Most stars spend some part of their lives in the main sequence which runs from top left to bottom right across the diagram. Giant stars are found above the main sequence and white dwarf stars below.

STAR FACTS

• Hot, bright young stars are found in large groups known as OB associations.

• By the standards of space, the Sun is very small. Astronomers refer to it as a type G dwarf star.

• The smallest stars, cooler and fainter than red dwarfs, are known as brown dwarfs.

BRIGHTNESS

HOW BRIGHTLY A STAR shines in the sky depends on its luminosity (amount of light energy produced), and on its distance from Earth. Astronomers use two different scales to measure a star's magnitude (brightness). Absolute magnitude compares stars from a standard distance. Apparent magnitude describes how bright a star appears as viewed from Earth.

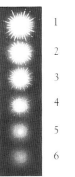

OBSERVED BRIGHTNESS
The scale of apparent magnitude for naked-eye stars. Brighter stars have lower numerical values.

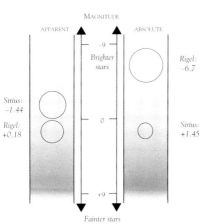

MAGNITUDE

APPARENT

ABSOLUTE

–9

Brighter stars

Rigel: –6.7

Sirius: –1.44

Rigel: +0.18

0

Sirius: +1.45

+9

Fainter stars

APPARENT VS ABSOLUTE
Sirius is the brightest star in our sky (apparent magnitude –1.46) brighter than Rigel (apparent magnitude +0.12). Yet in reality, Rigel is by far the brighter star with an absolute magnitude of –7.1, as opposed to Sirius which has an absolute magnitude of +1.4.

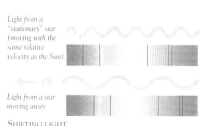

Light from a "stationary" star (moving with the same relative velocity as the Sun)

Light from a star moving away

BRIGHTNESS FACTS
• With both scales of magnitude, each whole number step (e.g. from +3 to +4) means that the star is $2\frac{1}{2}$ times brighter or fainter.
• The Sun's apparent magnitude is –26.7
• The brightest planet is Venus, with a maximum apparent magnitude of –4.7.

SHIFTING LIGHT

All objects in the universe are moving. In light from stars moving away from the Sun, the dark absorption lines are shifted toward the red end of the spectrum – the so-called "red shift."

HOW FAR?

Calculating a star's absolute magnitude means knowing its distance. For fairly close stars (within a few hundred light-years) astronomers can measure distance using the parallax method. Earth's orbit around the Sun enables astronomers to take two sightings of a star from opposite sides of the orbit. The apparent shift in position of the star between the two sightings is called the parallax. The greater the parallax, the nearer the star. In this case, star A has the greater shift and is the closer.

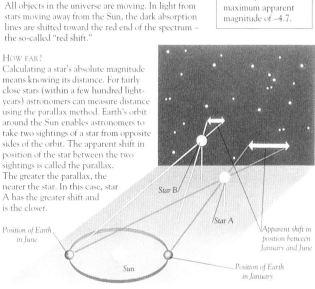

Star B

Star A

Apparent shift in position between January and June

Position of Earth in June

Position of Earth in January

Sun

SPACE FROM EARTH

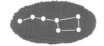

ABOVE OUR HEADS

OUR KNOWLEDGE of the universe has been gained from our unique position on Earth. By day the sky is dominated by the Sun. At night the blackness of space is studded with stars and galaxies which form an unchanging backdrop. However, our view of them changes throughout the year as Earth orbits the Sun.

CIRCULAR STAR TRAILS
Earth's daily rotation causes the stars to appear to circle around the sky. This effect can be captured by a long-exposure photograph.

Stars appear as patterns against the sphere.

CELESTIAL SPHERE
From Earth the stars appear to be set against a giant celestial sphere. As the Earth travels on its yearly orbit around the Sun, different sections of the sphere are exposed to our view. At any particular time, about half the sphere is hidden by the Sun's glare. The motion of other objects such as the planets, are also plotted against the sphere.

The Sun's path is called the ecliptic.

44

GALAXY

All the stars we
can see in the sky, including
the Sun, are in the Milky Way galaxy.
This panoramic view of the Milky
Way (looking towards the centre of
the galaxy), was photographed from
Christchurch, New Zealand.

MARTIAN MOTION

Planets, which have their own
orbits around the Sun, appear to
move across the sky against the
backdrop of stars. The name
"planet" is in fact taken from an
ancient Greek word meaning
"wanderer." Of all the planets,
Mars seems to wander the most –
sometimes it appears to change
direction and move backward
across Earth's sky. This backward
motion is in fact an optical
illusion caused by the Earth
overtaking Mars as it travels
around the Sun.

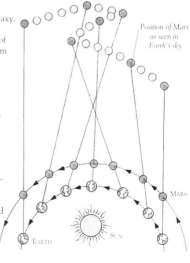

*Position of Mars
as seen in
Earth's sky*

EARTH

SUN

MARS

SPECIAL EFFECTS

FROM EARTH it is possible to see several "special effects" in the sky. Some of these effects are due to peculiarities of the Earth's magnetic field and atmosphere. Other effects depend on the position of the objects in the solar system, especially the Sun, Earth and Moon. Meteor showers are an effect produced by space dust burning up in the atmosphere.

AURORA BOREALIS
Charged particles from the Sun, carried by the solar wind, cause dramatic light shows when they enter Earth's atmosphere.

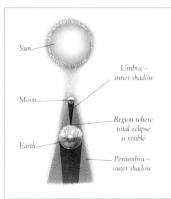

Sun

Umbra – inner shadow

Moon

Region where total eclipse is visible

Earth

Penumbra – outer shadow

ECLIPSE OF THE SUN
Occasionally, the Moon comes into perfect alignment between the Sun and the Earth. When this occurs, the Moon blocks out the Sun's light causing what is called a solar eclipse. From some parts of Earth's surface, the disc of the Moon appears to cover completely the Sun's face, and there is a brief period of darkness. Although the Moon is a great deal smaller than the Sun, it is able to block the light totally because it is so much nearer to the Earth.

HALO AROUND THE MOON

On some winter nights a halo appears around the Moon, but this has nothing to do with the Moon itself. Sunlight reflected toward Earth by the Moon is refracted (bent) by ice crystals high in Earth's atmosphere. This refraction of light creates a circular halo.

SPECIAL EFFECT FACTS

• Aurora borealis ("northern lights") are best observed from locations near the North Magnetic Pole. Similar displays in the Southern Hemisphere are called aurora australis.

• A lunar eclipse occurs when the Earth comes directly between the Sun and the Moon, and the Earth's shadow can be seen crossing the Moon's surface.

• A meteor radiant is an optical illusion. In fact, the meteors travel along parallel tracks.

METEOR RADIANT

Dust particles from space are seen as meteors when they burn up in the atmosphere. In a meteor shower, which is caused by dust from a comet, all the meteors appear to come from a single point in the sky. This point is known as the radiant of the meteor shower.

CONSTELLATIONS

SEEN FROM EARTH, the stars
seem to form patterns in the
sky. These patterns are known
as constellations. The skies
around Earth have been
divided into 88 different
constellations, each one of
which is supposed to represent
a mythological person,
creature, or object.

CONSTELLATION OF ORION
In Greek myth, Orion was a
mighty hunter. The row of
three bright stars (center left)
forms Orion's Belt, an
easily located
"skymark."

CELESTIAL
SPHERE
AS SEEN FROM
THE NORTHERN
HEMISPHERE

AROUND THE SPHERE
As the Earth makes its yearly orbit around
the Sun, different portions of the celestial
sphere come into view, presenting the
constellations in an annual sequence.

*Position of
Earth
in March*

*Constellations
visible from
Earth in March*

4 8

100,000 YEARS AGO

TODAY

100,000 YEARS FROM NOW

CHANGING SHAPE
The constellations appear fixed, but
in fact they change very slowly. The
changes to the Big Dipper can only
be seen over very long periods of time.

CONSTELLATION FACTS
• A constellation is a
two-dimensional view
of objects in three-
dimensional space.
• The Big Dipper is
not a separate
constellation but is
part of Ursa Major
(the Great Bear).
• The Aboriginal
people of Australia have
their own view of
constellations – they see
patterns in the dark
spaces between stars.

STARS IN THE
BIG DIPPER

Dubhe

Alkaid   Alioth   Megrez

Mizar   Phad   Merak

LINES OF SIGHT
The constellations are a
human invention. We see
them as flat patterns
against the blackness of
space, but in fact the stars
may be farther in distance
from each other than
they are from Earth. The
stars in the Big Dipper
seem to be close together.
However, they are more
scattered than they appear.

The Big
Dipper as seen
from Earth

Dubhe, the
farthest star, is
124 ly away;
Mizar, the nearest
star, is 78 ly
from Earth.

CATALOGING STARS

STARS ARE cataloged according to the constellation in which they appear. Within each constellation, the individual stars are identified by means of letters or numbers. Other objects are cataloged separately.

ORION

The constellation "figure" is drawn around the stars.

ORION NEBULA
In Earth's sky, the nebula appears as a faint, fuzzy patch of light just below Orion's Belt.

POSSESSIVE NAMES
All the constellations have been given Latin names. When referring to a particular star, the possessive case of the Latin name is used. For example, stars in the constellation of Orion are designated Orionis.

MAPPING THE SKIES
The constellations fit together to map the sky. All the stars inside a constellation's boundaries belong to that constellation, even if they appear to be unconnected to the star making up the main "title" figure.

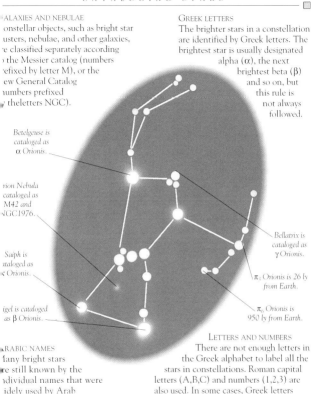

GALAXIES AND NEBULAE
...onstellar objects, such as bright star
...usters, nebulae, and other galaxies,
...e classified separately according
...o the Messier catalog (numbers
...refixed by letter M), or the
...ew General Catalog
...numbers prefixed
...y theletters NGC).

Betelgeuse is
cataloged as
α Orionis.

...rion Nebula
...cataloged as
...M42 and
...NGC1976.

Saiph is
...ataloged as
... Orionis.

...igel is cataloged
...as β Orionis.

GREEK LETTERS
The brighter stars in a constellation
are identified by Greek letters. The
brightest star is usually designated
alpha (α), the next
brightest beta (β)
and so on, but
this rule is
not always
followed.

Bellatrix is
cataloged as
γ Orionis.

π_3 Orionis is 26 ly
from Earth.

π_6 Orionis is
950 ly from Earth.

ARABIC NAMES
...1any bright stars
...re still known by the
...ndividual names that were
...idely used by Arab
...stronomers more than 800
...ears ago – e.g. Betelgeuse.
...aiph, and Rigel.

LETTERS AND NUMBERS
There are not enough letters in
the Greek alphabet to label all the
stars in constellations. Roman capital
letters (A,B,C) and numbers (1,2,3) are
also used. In some cases, Greek letters
are used with subscript numbers to
identify stars that are near to each other,
for example π_3 and π_6 Orionis.

THE ZODIAC

TWELVE CONSTELLATIONS ARE known as the zodiac.
These twelve are crossed by the ecliptic (the Sun's
annual path around the celestial sphere), and form
the backdrop for the movement of the Moon and
planets. The Sun spends about a month in each zodiac
constellation. Below are the dates when the Sun
actually enters each constellation – the zodiacal "signs"
of astrology are not the same as the constellations.

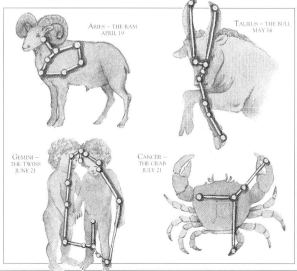

ARIES – THE RAM
APRIL 19

TAURUS – THE BULL
MAY 14

GEMINI –
THE TWINS
JUNE 21

CANCER –
THE CRAB
JULY 21

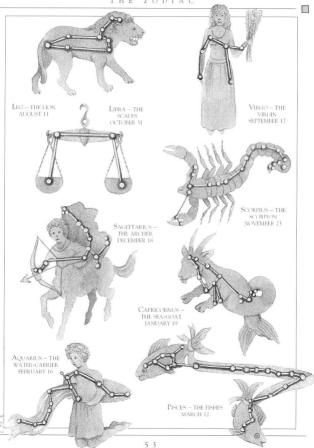

LEO – THE LION
AUGUST 11

LIBRA – THE
SCALES
OCTOBER 31

VIRGO – THE
VIRGIN
SEPTEMBER 17

SAGITTARIUS –
THE ARCHER
DECEMBER 18

SCORPIUS – THE
SCORPION
NOVEMBER 23

CAPRICORNUS –
THE SEA-GOAT
JANUARY 19

AQUARIUS – THE
WATER-CARRIER
FEBRUARY 16

PISCES – THE FISHES
MARCH 12

NEAR OR FAR?

STARS ARE VAST DISTANCES from us and from each other. Light, which travels faster than anything else, takes 8.3 minutes to travel from the Sun to the Earth. Light from the next nearest star, Proxima Centauri, takes 4.2 years. People cannot tell the distances to stars just by looking at them. But they can see subtle differences in color and apparent brightness.

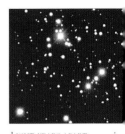

LIGHT-YEARS APART
All the stars in this distant cluster may look as if they are the same distance from Earth. Yet in fact the stars are many light-years apart.

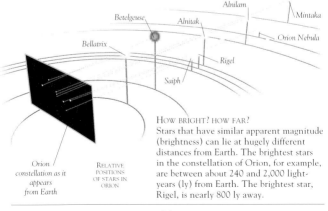

Alnilam

Mintaka

Betelgeuse

Alnitak

Orion Nebula

Bellatrix

Rigel

Saiph

Orion constellation as it appears from Earth

RELATIVE POSITIONS OF STARS IN ORION

HOW BRIGHT? HOW FAR?
Stars that have similar apparent magnitude (brightness) can lie at hugely different distances from Earth. The brightest stars in the constellation of Orion, for example, are between about 240 and 2,000 light-years (ly) from Earth. The brightest star, Rigel, is nearly 800 ly away.

STELLAR DATA: NEAREST STARS TO THE SUN

Name	Distance	Color
Proxima Centauri	4.2 ly	red
α Centauri A	4.4 ly	yellow
α Centauri B	4.4 ly	orange
Barnard's Star	5.9 ly	red
Wolf 359	7.8 ly	red
Lalande 21185	8.3 ly	red
Sirius A	8.6 ly	white
Sirius B	8.6 ly	white

STAR FACTS

• Proxima Centauri is part of a triple star system along with α Centauri A and α Centauri B.

• The brightest star, Sirius A, has a faint white dwarf companion Sirius B.

NEIGHBOURING STARS

Many of the stars within 40 light-years of the Sun are dim red dwarfs like Barnard's Star, which cannot be seen with the naked eye. Others, such as Vega, are 50 times more luminous than the Sun.

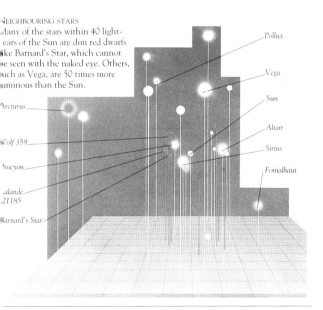

Pollux

Vega

Sun

Arcturus

Altair

Wolf 359

Sirius

Procyon

Fomalhaut

Lalande 21185

Barnard's Star

THE NORTHERN SKY

AT RIGHT ARE THE MAIN STARS that lie north of the celestial equator. The stars seen on a particular night by people living in the northern hemisphere depend on the observer's latitude, the time of year, and the time of night. The stars near the center of the sky-map are called circumpolar and can be seen throughout the year. Polaris (the North Star) appears to remain directly over the North Pole.

Arcturus

North celestial pole

PROJECTED SPHERE
This sky-map is a projection of the northern half of the celestial sphere onto a flat surface. Earth's North Pole is situated directly below the center of the map. The celestial equator is a projection of Earth's equator out into space.

Celestial equator

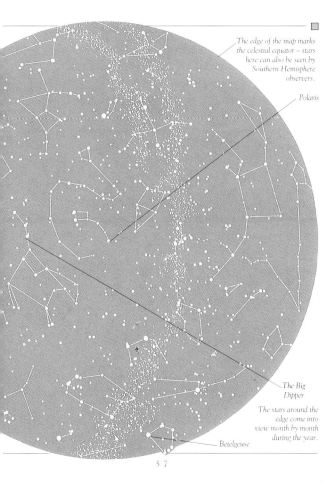

The edge of the map marks the celestial equator – stars here can also be seen by Southern Hemisphere observers.

Polaris

The Big Dipper

The stars around the edge come into view month by month during the year.

Betelgeuse

THE SOUTHERN SKY

AT RIGHT ARE THE MAIN STARS that lie south
of the celestial equator. The stars seen on a
particular night by people living in the southern
hemisphere depend on the observer's latitude,
the time of year, and the time of night.
The stars near the center of the sky-map
are called circumpolar and can be seen
all year round. Alpha Centauri, one
of the nearest stars to the Sun, is
a southern hemisphere star.

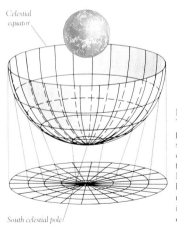

Celestial equator

Alpha Centauri

Antares

PROJECTED SPHERE
This sky-map is a
projection of the
southern half of the
celestial sphere onto a
flat surface. Earth's South
Pole is situated directly
below the center of the
map. The celestial equator
is a projection of Earth's
equator out into space.

South celestial pole

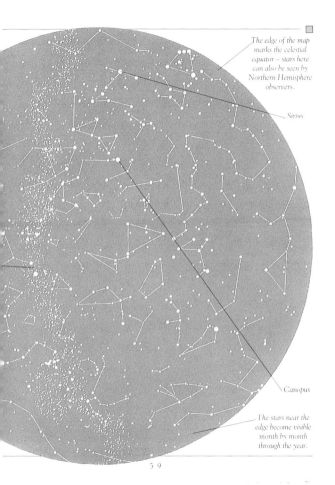

The edge of the map marks the celestial equator – stars here can also be seen by Northern Hemisphere observers.

Sirius

Canopus

The stars near the edge become visible month by month through the year.

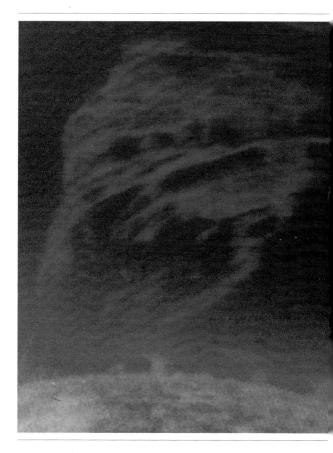

SOLAR
SYSTEM

WHAT IS THE SOLAR SYSTEM?

THE SOLAR SYSTEM consists of the Sun and the many objects that orbit around it – nine planets, more than 100 moons, and countless asteroids and comets. The system occupies a disk-shaped volume of space more than 7.45 billion miles (12 billion kilometers) across. At the center is the Sun which contains more than 99 percent of the solar system's mass.

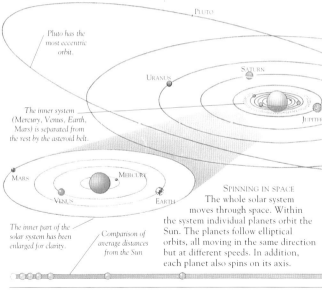

PLUTO

Pluto has the most eccentric orbit.

URANUS

SATURN

JUPITER

The inner system (Mercury, Venus, Earth, Mars) is separated from the rest by the asteroid belt.

MARS

MERCURY

VENUS

EARTH

The inner part of the solar system has been enlarged for clarity.

Comparison of average distances from the Sun

SPINNING IN SPACE
The whole solar system moves through space. Within the system individual planets orbit the Sun. The planets follow elliptical orbits, all moving in the same direction but at different speeds. In addition, each planet also spins on its axis.

MERCURY

VENUS

EARTH

MARS

JUPITER

SATURN

URANUS

NEPTUNE

NEPTUNE

PLUTO

- Images obtained with the latest telescopes strongly suggest that some other stars (e.g. β Pictoris) are forming planetary systems.

- The solar system has more than 100 moons by the latest count. Future space probes are almost certain to discover extra moons orbiting the outer planets.

Each of the four gas planets has a ring system around it – the rings have been omitted from this illustration for ease of comparison.

Orbits are elliptical rather than circular

The time taken for a planet to make one orbit of the Sun is called the orbital period.

Pluto is the smallest and least-known planet.

NINE PLANETS

The planets form two main groups – the inner four are composed of rock, while the next four are larger and are composed mostly of liquefied gas. The outermost planet, Pluto, is composed of rock and ice.

SOLAR GRAVITY

ABOUT 4.6 BILLION years ago, the solar system formed
from a cloud of gas and dust. The Sun formed first and
the other objects formed from
the leftovers. The Sun's
gravity dominates the
system because it is so
massive by comparison
with the planets.

CONDENSING INTO PLACE
The young Sun was surrounded
by a disk of dust, gas, and
snow. Dust clumped
together to form the four
inner rock planets. The
giant outer planets formed
from a mixture of gas, snow,
and dust. Pluto and the comets
formed from the icy leftovers.

ORBITAL PATHS
Most of the planets orbit close to the plane of
the Earth's orbit (the ecliptic). Pluto has the
most inclined orbit, possibly because it is the
most distant planet and is the least influenced
by the Sun's gravity. However the next most
inclined planet is Mercury (7°),
which is the nearest
planet to the Sun.

THE PLANETS:
ORBITAL INCLINATION
TO THE ECLIPTIC

Pluto: 17.2°
Mercury: 7°
Venus: 3.39°
Saturn: 2.49°
Mars: 1.85°
Neptune: 1.77°
Jupiter: 1.3°
Uranus: 0.77°
Earth: 0°

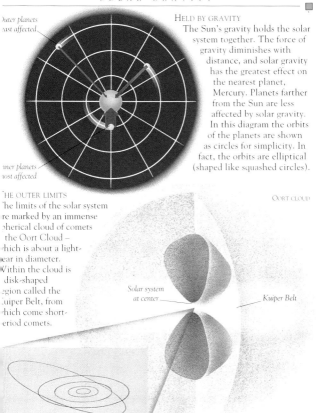

Outer planets
least affected

Inner planets
most affected

HELD BY GRAVITY

The Sun's gravity holds the solar system together. The force of gravity diminishes with distance, and solar gravity has the greatest effect on the nearest planet, Mercury. Planets farther from the Sun are less affected by solar gravity. In this diagram the orbits of the planets are shown as circles for simplicity. In fact, the orbits are elliptical (shaped like squashed circles).

THE OUTER LIMITS

The limits of the solar system are marked by an immense spherical cloud of comets – the Oort Cloud – which is about a light-year in diameter. Within the cloud is a disk-shaped region called the Kuiper Belt, from which come short-period comets.

OORT CLOUD

Solar system at center

Kuiper Belt

THE SUN

LIKE OTHER STARS, the Sun is
a huge ball of spinning gas.
Nuclear reactions take place
at its core, giving off energy.
The Sun is the only star close
enough to be studied in detail.
Its surface features, such as
sunspots and prominences,
can be observed from Earth.
Satellites and space probes are
able to get a closer view and
obtain even more information.

ECLIPSE OF THE SUN
During an eclipse, the outer
layer of the Sun, the corona,
becomes visible. Normally
the corona is hidden by glare.

| Year 1 | Year 4 | Year 7 | Year 10 | Year 12 |

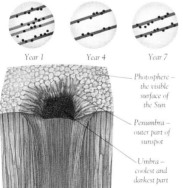

Photosphere –
the visible
surface of
the Sun

Penumbra –
outer part of
sunspot

Umbra –
coolest and
darkest part

COOL AND DARK
Sunspots, dark patches on the
surface, are regions of cooler gas
caused by disturbances in the
Sun's magnetic field. Sunspots
follow an 11-year cycle that
begins with the Sun being spot-
free. The spots appear at high
latitude and gradually increase
in number, moving toward the
Sun's equator during the cycle.

SOLAR DATA

Average distance from Earth	93,026,724 miles
	(149,680,000 km)
Distance from center of galaxy	30,000 light-years
Diameter (at equator)	865,121 miles
	(1,391,980 km)
Rotation period (at equator)	25.04 Earth days
Mass (Earth = 1)	330,000
Gravity (Earth = 1)	27.9
Average density (water = 1)	1.41
Absolute magnitude	4.83

SOLAR FACTS

• **Never look directly at the Sun. Even with sunglasses, camera film, or smoked glass you risk damaging your eyesight.**

• The safe way is to project the Sun's image onto a piece of paper using a hand lens.

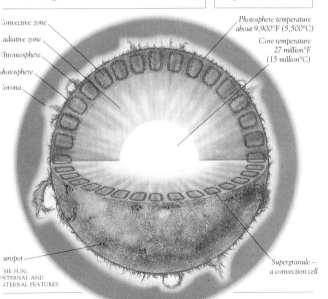

Convective zone

Radiative zone

Chromosphere

Photosphere

Corona

Photosphere temperature about 9,900°F (5,500°C)

Core temperature 27 million°F (15 million°C)

Sunspot

THE SUN: EXTERNAL AND INTERNAL FEATURES

Supergranule – a convection cell

SOLAR ENERGY AND INFLUENCE

AT ITS CORE, the Sun converts hydrogen to helium at rate of 600 million tons (tonne every second. The energy produced eventually reaches the surface and travels through space.

Visible light and other radiation travels from the Sun's surface to Earth in about 8 minutes.

Nuclear reactions at core produce gamma rays

Gamma rays take up to two million years to travel to surface, losing energy in the process

SOLAR PROMINENCES
Enormous jets of hot gas shoot out from the Sun's surface stretching for many thousands of miles (kilometers). The largest jets, called prominences can last for several months. Th Sun's magnetic field holds som prominences in gigantic loops.

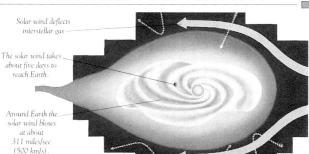

Solar wind deflects interstellar gas

The solar wind takes about five days to reach Earth.

Around Earth the solar wind blows at about 311 miles/sec (500 km/s).

Solar wind deflects most cosmic rays

EXTENT OF INFLUENCE

The Sun influences an enormous volume of space around it. Gases streaming from the corona become the high-speed solar wind. The solar wind carries a magnetic field from the Sun. As the Sun rotates, the field takes on a spiral shape. The volume of space swept by the solar wind is called the heliosphere.

ULYSSES
SOLAR PROBE

Sensors located on hinged boom

TO THE SOLAR POLES

Earth's orbit in the Sun's equatorial plane means that the Sun's poles cannot be studied from Earth. The Ulysses probe was launched in 1990 to study these hard-to-observe regions.

SOLAR ENERGY FACTS

• Converting hydrogen to helium means that the Sun loses four million tons (tonnes) of its mass every second.

• The amount of the Sun's energy reaching Earth's atmosphere (known as the solar constant) is equivalent to 1.37 kw (kilowatts) of electricity per square meter.

PLANETS

MERCURY

A SMALL ROCK WORLD with a large dense core, Mercury is the closest planet to the Sun. There is no real atmosphere, and much of the surface is marked by numerous impact craters. Dominated by the Sun, Mercury experiences the greatest variation in surface temperature of any planet in the solar system. Differences between day and night can be more than 1,080°F (600°C).

DIFFICULT TO SEE
Photographs taken from Earth show Mercury as a fuzzy disk, difficult to observe against the Sun. This image was put together from photographs taken by the Mariner 10 probe.

Earth

Mercury

MERCURY: PLANETARY DATA	
Average distance from the Sun	36 million miles (57.9 million km)
Orbital period	88 Earth days
Orbital velocity	29.7 miles/sec (47.9 km/s)
Rotation period	58.7 Earth days
Diameter at equator	3,032 miles (4,879 km)
Surface temperature	–292°F to +806°F (–180°C to +430°C)
Mass (Earth = 1)	0.055
Gravity (Earth = 1)	0.38
Number of moons	0

MERCURY FACTS

• Mercury was named after the fleet-footed messenger of the Roman gods because it travels so quickly across Earth's sky.

• Mercury's largest crater, Caloris Planitia, measures 875 miles (1,400 km) across.

42% oxygen

29% sodium

22% hydrogen

6% helium

MERCURY:
COMPOSITION OF ATMOSPHERE

THIN AIR

Mercury's atmosphere is extremely thin – less than one trillionth of Earth's. Sodium and potassium occur in the daytime only, as the Sun's energy releases them from the planet's surface.

PROBE'S EYE VIEW
Craters cover about 60 percent of Mercury's surface. The other 40 percent consists of relatively smooth plains.

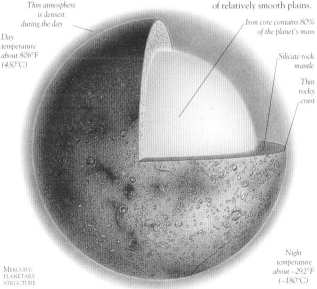

Thin atmosphere is densest during the day

Day temperature about 806°F (430°C)

Iron core contains 80% of the planet's mass

Silicate rock mantle

Thin rocky crust

MERCURY:
PLANETARY
STRUCTURE

Night temperature about –292°F (–180°C)

LONG DAYS

Mercury rotates very slowly
on an upright axis at 90° to
the plane of its orbit. A single
day on Mercury (sunrise to
sunrise) lasts for 176 Earth days.
Although days are very long, the
Mercurian year is very short. Mercury
takes only 88 Earth days to complete
one orbit around the Sun. This is the
shortest obital period of all the planets.

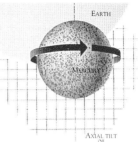

EARTH

MERCURY

AXIAL TILT
0°

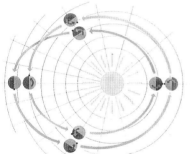

ECCENTRIC ORBIT

A combination of long days
and short years would create
strange effects for any
inhabitants. While
Mercury completes two
orbits of the Sun (shown
here separately for clarity),
an observer on the surface
(marked by a dot) would
experience only one Mercurian
day. Birthdays would happen
more often than sunrise.

SURFACE MAP
The Mariner 10
photographs were
used to produce
maps of Mercury.
Each square of the
grid covers about
50 x 50 miles
(80 x 80 km).

IMPACT CRATER FORMATION ON ROCK PLANETS

A meteorite impact blasts out a circular crater, and ejected material falls back to form a circular rim.

Rock compressed by the initial impact may bounce back from the sides to form a roughly conical central peak.

The crater profile is gradually reduced as rock fragments and debris slip from the walls and peak.

SOLITARY VISITOR

Mariner 10 is the only probe to have made a detailed study of Mercury. Launched in November 1973, the probe took five months to reach the planet. During three close approaches the probe photographed about 40 percent of the surface area. At its closest approach, Mariner 10 was 187 miles (300 km) above the surface.

High resolution cameras

MARINER 10 PROBE

MERCURY: CREATIVE CRATER NAMES

Mercury's craters commemorate creative people:

Writers	Composers	Painters	Architects
Bronte	Bach	Brueghel	Bernini
Cervantes	Chopin	Cezanne	Bramante
Dickens	Grieg	Dürer	Imhotep
Goethe	Handel	Holbein	Mansart
Li Po	Liszt	Monet	Michelangelo
Melville	Mozart	Renoir	Sinan
Shelley	Stravinsky	Titian	Sullivan
Tolstoy	Verdi	Van Gogh	Wren

FACTS

• Mercury can only be seen from Earth at twilight – either just before dawn or just after sunset.

• Parts of Mercury's surface have a wrinkled appearance – the result of the planet shrinking as its core cooled.

VENUS

A ROCK PLANET with a dense
atmosphere, Venus is almost
the same size as the Earth.
The two share some surface
features, but conditions on
Venus are very different from
those on Earth. The surface
environment of Venus is
extremely hostile – intense
heat, crushing pressure, and
unbreathable air. Overhead
there are thick clouds of
sulfuric acid droplets.

OBSCURED BY CLOUDS
The surface features of Venus
are hidden by a permanent
blanket of thick cloud. The
dark swirls are high-altitude
wind systems.

Venus

Earth

VENUS: PLANETARY DATA	
Average distance from the Sun	67.2 million miles (108.2 million km)
Orbital period	224.7 Earth days
Orbital velocity	21.7 miles/sec (35 km/s)
Rotation period	243 Earth days
Diameter at equator	7,521 miles (12,104 km)
Surface temperature	860°F (460°C)
Mass (Earth = 1)	0.81
Gravity (Earth = 1)	0.91
Number of moons	0

VENUS FACTS

• Venus shines brightly
in Earth's sky because
the cloud layer reflects
most of the sunlight.

• Venus has phases like
the Moon. You need a
telescope to see them
clearly, but binoculars
will enable you to see
the crescent phase.

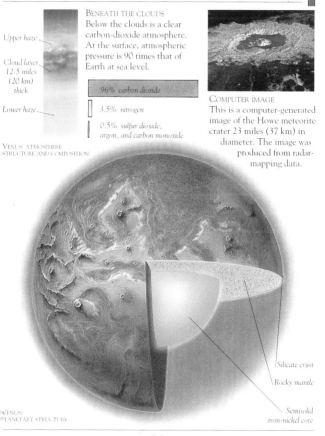

Upper haze

Cloud layer 12.5 miles (20 km) thick

Lower haze

VENUS: ATMOSPHERE STRUCTURE AND COMPOSITION

BENEATH THE CLOUDS

Below the clouds is a clear carbon-dioxide atmosphere. At the surface, atmospheric pressure is 90 times that of Earth at sea level.

96% carbon dioxide

3.5% nitrogen

0.5% sulfur dioxide, argon, and carbon monoxide

COMPUTER IMAGE

This is a computer-generated image of the Howe meteorite crater 23 miles (37 km) in diameter. The image was produced from radar-mapping data.

VENUS: PLANETARY STRUCTURE

Silicate crust

Rocky mantle

Semisolid iron-nickel core

BACKWARD ROTATION

Venus is one of only three planets to rotate on its axis in a backward direction (the others are Pluto and Uranus). Venus' backward rotation is so slow that a Venusian day lasts longer (243 Earth days) than a Venusian year (224.7 Earth days). Driven by powerful winds, Venus' atmosphere moves at its own, much faster, pace. The upper levels of the cloud layer take just four Earth days to travel right around the planet.

AXIAL TILT
2°

EARTH

VENUS

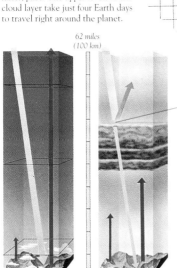

62 miles
(100 km)

Sunlight reflected by cloud layer

EARTH

VENUS

GREENHOUSE PLANET

Venus has a higher average surface temperature (860°F/460°C) than any other planet in the solar system. The heating of Venus is the result of a "greenhouse effect" run wild. Although the cloud layer reflects much of the sunlight that hits it, some solar heat energy does reach the surface. But instead of being radiated back into space, this heat energy is trapped by the cloud layer causing temperatures to rise. On Earth the cloud layer allows much more heat to escape.

MAGELLAN PROBE

Solar panels

Propulsion module

Radar signal reflected by surface features

Radio signal measures altitude

AERIAL VIEW
Maat Mons is an extinct volcano about 5 miles (8 km) high. This image was produced by the Magellan probe's radar-mapping techniques that can penetrate Venus' thick clouds. The data has been processed to give a viewpoint located about 1 mile (1.6 km) above the planet's surface.

VENUS: SELECTED EXPLORATION EVENTS		
Probe	Date	Result
Mariner 2	14/12/62	Successful flyby
Venera 4	18/10/67	Sampled atmosphere
Venera 7	15/12/70	Sent data from surface
Mariner 10	5/2/74	Flyby on way to Mercury
Venera 9	23/10/75	First orbit and soft landing and first surface image
Venera 15	10/10/83	First radar mapping
Pioneer-Venus 2	9/12/78	Multiple descent probes investigate atmosphere
Magellan	10/8/90	Complete radar mapping

MORE FACTS
• The facts that Venus has a small axial tilt and backward rotation is just popular convention. According to the rules of the IAU (International Astronomical Union), Venus rotates in a normal direction around an axis tilted at 177.4° to the vertical.

EARTH

THE THIRD PLANET from the
Sun, Earth, is unique in the
solar system and is possibly
unique in the universe.
Only Earth has the surface
conditions that permit
liquid water to exist, and
Earth alone has developed
an oxygen-rich atmosphere.
These two factors have
enabled the rocky planet
Earth to evolve myriad
varieties of life.

JEWEL IN SPACE
Photographed by Apollo
astronauts returning from the
Moon, planet Earth looks like a
brightly colored jewel – blue
oceans, white clouds, and green-
brown land masses.

Earth

EARTH: PLANETARY DATA	
Average distance from the Sun	93 million miles (149.6 million km)
Orbital period	365.25 days
Orbital velocity	18.5 miles/sec (29.8 km/s)
Rotation period	23.93 hours
Diameter at equator	7,926 miles (12,756 km)
Surface temperature	–94°F to +131°F (–70°C to +55°C)
Gravity (Earth = 1)	1
Number of moons	1

EARTH FACTS
• The oldest rocks so
far discovered in the
Earth's crust date back
3.9 billion years.
• The oxygen in
Earth's atmosphere is
the result of life. The
process of oxygenation
began with bacteria
about 2 billion years
ago.

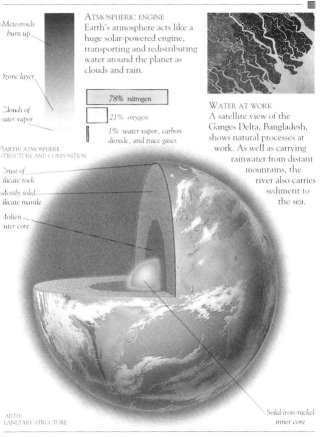

ATMOSPHERIC ENGINE
Earth's atmosphere acts like a
huge solar-powered engine,
transporting and redistributing
water around the planet as
clouds and rain.

| 78% nitrogen |
| 21% oxygen |
| 1% water vapor, carbon dioxide, and trace gases |

Meteoroids
burn up

Ozone layer

Clouds of
water vapor

EARTH: ATMOSPHERE
STRUCTURE AND COMPOSITION

WATER AT WORK
A satellite view of the
Ganges Delta, Bangladesh,
shows natural processes at
work. As well as carrying
rainwater from distant
mountains, the
river also carries
sediment to
the sea.

Crust of
silicate rock

Mostly solid
silicate mantle

Molten
outer core

EARTH:
PLANETARY STRUCTURE

Solid iron-nickel
inner core

UNEQUAL HEATING

Earth's axis of rotation is tilted at 23.5° to the vertical. As the planet travels around the Sun during the year, the tilt causes seasonal variations in climate. These variations are most noticeable in the high latitudes away from the equator. Spinning on a tilted axis gives rise to unequal heating of the surface by the Sun. This differential heating produces differences in atmospheric pressure which create the wind systems that drive Earth's climate.

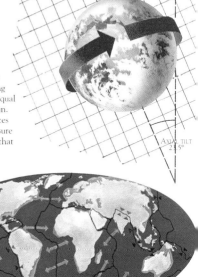

AXIAL TILT
23.5°

200 MYA

60 MYA

200 MILLION YEARS AGO
The continents were grouped closer together.

60 MILLION YEARS AGO
The landmasses had moved some way toward their present locations.

CONTINENTS IN MOTION
The continents "float" on the surface of the Earth's crust, which is made up of a number of separate plates. These plates are in constant slow-motion, pushed apart as new crust is produced at mid-ocean ridges. The result is that the continents are also gradually moving. Areas where plates are in collision have many volcanoes and earthquakes.

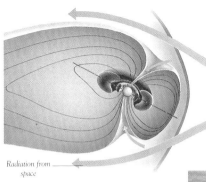

Radiation from
space

SPINNING MAGNET

Earth has a much stronger magnetic field than any of the other rock planets. Produced by the rapid rotation of the nickel-iron core, the magnetic field extends far into space and deflects harmful radiation away from the planet. Despite its elongated ovoid shape, this magnetic field is called the magnetosphere.

THE WATER OF LIFE

Water only exists in its liquid form between 32°F (0°C) and 212°F (100°C), which is about the same range of temperatures found on Earth. Liquid water is absolutely essential to practically all forms of life. Along with carbon dioxide, it is one of the two raw materials used by plants to produce their own food and provide the oxygen upon which animal life depends.

EARTH: PHYSICAL LIMITS	
Age	4.6 billion years
Mass	6,571 million million million tons
Surface area	317 million sq miles
	(510 million km²)
Covered by water	70.8 percent
Highest mountain	29,028 ft (8,848 meters)
Deepest ocean trench	35,800 ft (10,924 meters)
Oldest evidence of life	3.5 billion years ago
Total number of living species	at least 10 million

MORE FACTS

• The Atlantic Ocean increases in width by about 1.2 in (3 cm) each year.

• Earth has periodic magnetic reversals when the north pole becomes the south pole, and the south becomes north.

EARTH'S MOON

EARTH HAS A single satellite, the Moon, which is about one-quarter the size of our planet. Although the Earth and the Moon are closely linked, there are many striking contrasts. The Moon is a waterless, airless, and lifeless place. Its surface is covered by craters, the scars of a massive meteorite bombardment that took place billions of years ago.

FAMILIAR SIGHT
Some of the features on the Moon can be identified with the naked eye. Binoculars, or a small telescope, will reveal a considerable amount of detail.

The Moon's distance from Earth varies during its orbit.

Minimum   Average   Maximum

THE MOON: DATA	
Average distance from the Earth	238,855 miles (384,400 km)
Orbital period	27.3 Earth days
Orbital velocity	0.6 miles/sec (1 km/s)
Rotation period	27.3 Earth days
Diameter at equator	2,159 miles (3,475 km)
Surface temperature	–247°F to +221°F (–155°C to +105°C)
Mass (Earth = 1)	0.012
Gravity (Earth = 1)	0.16
Escape velocity	1.48 miles/sec (2.38 km/s)

MOON FACTS

• The Moon has approximately the same surface area as the continents of North and South America.

• The pull of the Moon's gravity is largely responsible for the twice daily rise and fall of tides in Earth's seas and oceans.

FIGURE IN A MOONSCAPE
The Moon remains unique as the only
extraterrestrial object upon which
human beings have walked. Protected
by a spacesuit from the airless lunar
environment, one of the Apollo 17
astronauts investigates a large boulder.
Undisturbed by the effects of wind or
rain, his footprints should remain
visible for millions of years.

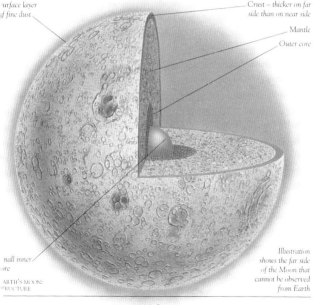

Surface layer
of fine dust

Crust – thicker on far
side than on near side

Mantle

Outer core

Small inner
core

EARTH'S MOON:
STRUCTURE

*Illustration
shows the far side
of the Moon that
cannot be observed
from Earth*

HELD IN PLACE

Earth is larger and more massive than the Moon, and has a powerful effect on its smaller neighbor. Under the influence of Earth's gravity the Moon's motion through space has been moderated so that its rotation period is the same as its orbital period – 27.3 days. This synchronization of motion means that the same face of the Moon is always turned toward the Earth – the near side. The other side is always turned away from us – the far side.

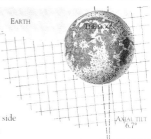

EARTH

THE MOON

AXIAL TILT 6.7°

BATTERED SURFACE

About 3.8 billion years ago, the Moon's surface received an intense meteorite bombardment.

Some 1 billion years later, the largest craters gradually filled up with dark lava, and formed the lunar seas.

Since that time, the appearance of the lunar surface has hardly changed apart from a few recent ray craters.

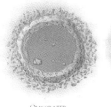

OLD CRATER

RAY CRATER

CHANGING MOONSCAPE

Most of the craters were made about 4 billion years ago, and many are only faintly visible. Some newer craters are identifiable by conspicuous rays of pale ejected material fanning out from the crater wall.

MOON ROCK

About 836 lb (380 kg) of moon rock have been brought back to Earth. There are no sedimentary or metamorphic rocks on the Moon – all the samples brought back are either igneous lavas (mainly basalt) or breccias produced by the heat and force of meteorite impacts. Most of the Moon's surface is covered with a layer of crushed and broken rock (called "regolith") which is about 65 ft (20 m) deep.

MOON ROCK COLLECTED BY APOLLO ASTRONAUTS

PHASES OF THE MOON

The Moon shines by reflected sunlight. As it travels around the Earth, the visible amount of sunlit area changes day by day. Viewed from Earth's surface, this produces a cycle of lunar phases – waxing from New Moon to Full Moon, and then waning back to New Moon once more.

Waning

SUNLIGHT

Full Moon

New Moon

Waxing

EARTH'S MOON: SELECTED EXPLORATION EVENTS		
Vehicle	Date	Result
Luna 3	10/10/59	First images of far side
Luna 9	3/2/66	First soft landing
Surveyor 3	17/4/67	Landing site soil studies
Apollo 11	20/7/69	Humans first land on Moon
Luna 16	24/9/70	Robot returns with samples
Luna 17	17/11/70	Mobile robot landed
Apollo 15	30/7/71	Lunar Roving Vehicle used
Apollo 17	11/12/72	Last Apollo mission lands

MORE FACTS

• The first person to step on to the Moon was the astronaut Neil Armstrong early on July 21, 1969.

• His historic first words were, " That's one small step for a man, one giant leap for mankind."

MARS

A RED-HUED ROCKY PLANET,
Mars is a cold, barren world
with a thin atmosphere. There
are many Earthlike features,
such as polar ice caps and water-
carved valleys, but there are
many important differences.
Temperatures rarely rise above
the freezing point, the air is
unbreathable, and dust-storms
occasionally scour the surface.
The planet's red color is caused
by the presence of iron oxide.

LONG RANGE VIEW
This image was obtained by the
Earth-orbiting Hubble Space
Telescope at a distance of about
43 million miles (69 million
km) from Mars. Bluish clouds
can be seen near the poles.

Earth

Mars

MARS: PLANETARY DATA	
Average distance from the Sun	141.6 million miles (227.9 million km)
Orbital period	687 Earth days
Orbital velocity	15 miles/sec (24.1 km/s)
Rotation period	24.62 hours
Diameter at equator	4,220 miles (6,792 km)
Surface temperature	–184°F to +77°F (–120°C to +25°C)
Mass (Earth = 1)	0.107
Gravity (Earth = 1)	0.38
Moons:	2

MARS FACTS

• Mars was named
after the Roman god
of war because it
appears the color of
spilled blood.

• The south polar ice
cap on Mars is much
larger than the north
polar ice cap, and the
southern winter is
considerably longer.

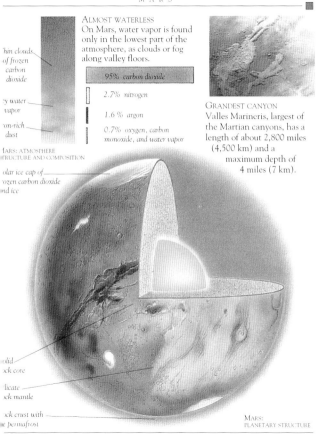

ALMOST WATERLESS
On Mars, water vapor is found only in the lowest part of the atmosphere, as clouds or fog along valley floors.

95% carbon dioxide
2.7% nitrogen
1.6 % argon
0.7% oxygen, carbon monoxide, and water vapor

Thin clouds of frozen carbon dioxide

Dry water vapor

Iron-rich dust

MARS: ATMOSPHERE STRUCTURE AND COMPOSITION

GRANDEST CANYON
Valles Marineris, largest of the Martian canyons, has a length of about 2,800 miles (4,500 km) and a maximum depth of 4 miles (7 km).

Polar ice cap of frozen carbon dioxide and ice

Solid rock core

Silicate rock mantle

Rock crust with permafrost

MARS:
PLANETARY STRUCTURE

EARTHLIKE SEASONS
Mars is smaller than
the Earth, but turns
on its axis more
slowly, so that the
day lengths are almost
identical. A day on
Mars is just 41 minutes
longer. A similar axial
tilt gives Mars the same
pattern of seasons as we
experience on Earth. However,
because of the greater orbital
period (687 Earth days), the length
of each season is nearly twice as long.

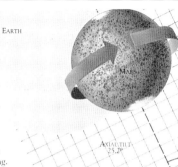

EARTH

MARS

AXIAL TILT
25.2°

DESERT SURFACE
This is a view of the Martian surface
photographed by the Mars Pathfinder
lander. Part of the lander is seen here in
the foreground. The hills on the horizon,
nicknamed Twin Peaks, are 0.6-1.2 miles
(1-2 km) away. This "stony desert"
appearance is typical of about 40 percent
of Mars' surface. Some Martian landforms,
however, are more dramatic. Olympus
Mons towers 13 miles (21 km) high.

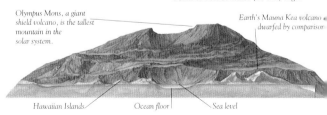

Olympus Mons, a giant
shield volcano, is the tallest
mountain in the
solar system.

Earth's Mauna Kea volcano
dwarfed by comparison

Hawaiian Islands

Ocean floor

Sea level

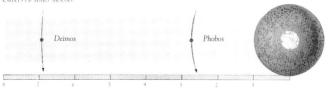

Deimos

Phobos

SCALE IN RADIUSES OF MARS

SMALL MOONS

Mars has two tiny moons, Phobos
and Deimos, neither of them more
than 18.5 miles (30 km) in length.
Both are irregularly shaped and have
every appearance of being asteroids
that were captured by Mars' gravity.
Phobos orbits Mars at a distance of
5,827 miles (9,378 km) every 7 hours
and 40 minutes. Deimos orbits three
times farther away, at a distance of
14,577 miles (23,459 km), and takes
about 30 hours to circle the planet.

*Smaller and darker
than its companion*

DEIMOS

PHOBOS

*The crater
Stickney is
nearly 6.2 miles
(10 km)
across.*

MARS: SELECTED EXPLORATION EVENTS		
Vehicle	Date	Result
Mariner 4	14/7/65	First flyby images
Mariner 9	13/11/71	First Mars orbiter
Mars 3	2/12/71	Orbit achieved, lander failed after 20 seconds
Viking 1 & Viking 2	20/7/76 3/9/76	Provided images and soil analysis
Mars Pathfinder	4/7/97	Lander carrying Sojourner micro-rover
Mars Global Surveyor	11/9/97	Orbiter, mapped and measured surface detail

MORE FACTS

• Phobos means "fear,"
and Deimos means
"terror" – suitable
companions for the
planet named after a
god of war.

• Viewed from the
surface of Mars, Phobos
crosses the sky three
times each day.

JUPITER

THE LARGEST of the planets, Jupiter has two and a half times more mass than all the other planets together. Jupiter has a small rock core, but consists mainly of gas in various physical states. The mantle of cold liquefied gas merges into a dense atmosphere. Giant wind systems give Jupiter a banded appearance.

GAS GIANT
The Cassini probe took this image from a distance of 48.2 million miles (77.6 million km). The patterns are caused by rising and falling regions of gas in the atmosphere.

Earth   Jupiter

JUPITER: PLANETARY DATA	
Average distance from the Sun	483.7 million miles (778.4 million km)
Orbital period	11.86 Earth years
Orbital velocity	8.1 miles/sec (13.1 km/s)
Rotation period	9.84 hours
Diameter at equator	88,846 miles (142,984 km)
Cloud-top temperature	−238°F (−150°C)
Mass (Earth = 1)	318
Gravity (Earth = 1)	2.54
Number of moons	40

JUPITER FACTS

• The pressure in Jupiter's interior is so great that hydrogen gas exists naturally in a semisolid metallic form not yet made on Earth.

• Jupiter can be seen with the naked eye as a bright silver "star" in Earth's night sky.

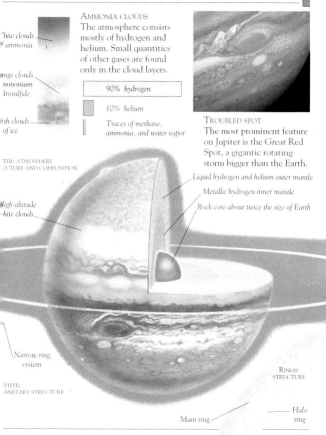

AMMONIA CLOUDS
The atmosphere consists mostly of hydrogen and helium. Small quantities of other gases are found only in the cloud layers.

White clouds of ammonia

Orange clouds of ammonium hydrosulfide

Bluish clouds of ice

| 90% hydrogen |

10% helium

Traces of methane, ammonia, and water vapor

JUPITER: ATMOSPHERE
STRUCTURE AND COMPOSITION

TROUBLED SPOT
The most prominent feature on Jupiter is the Great Red Spot, a gigantic rotating storm bigger than the Earth.

Liquid hydrogen and helium outer mantle

Metallic hydrogen inner mantle

Rock core about twice the size of Earth

High-altitude white clouds

Narrow ring system

JUPITER:
PLANETARY STRUCTURE

RINGS:
STRUCTURE

Halo ring

Main ring

FASTEST SPINNER

Despite its enormous size, 11 times the diameter of Earth, Jupiter rotates on its axis faster than any other planet. This high-speed rotation causes the gas giant to bulge around the equator, giving it a slightly oval shape. The rapid rotation also produces the powerful wind systems which divide Jupiter's atmosphere into bands that lie parallel with the equator. The most powerful winds move at speeds of several hundred miles (kilometers) per hour.

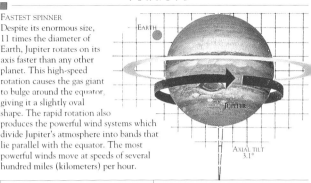

EARTH

JUPITER

AXIAL TILT
3.1°

THE GALILEAN MOONS:

EUROPA
Covered by a smooth layer of solid ice, Europa has sufficient internal heat to have seas of liquid water lying beneath its featureless surface.

CALLISTO
Covered with cracked and dirty ice around a rock core, Callisto is scarred by many craters. The largest is named Valhalla, with a diameter of 1,865 miles (3,000 km).

GANYMEDE
The largest moon in the solar system, Ganymede is larger than the planets Pluto and Mercury. Believed to consist mainly of ice and slush, Ganymede may have a silicate rock core.

IO
Debris from many volcanoes gives Io's surface an orange color. The interior is still molten, and Io has the first active volcanoes to be discovered outside the Earth.

MOONS OF JUPITER

The four largest moons were discovered by Galileo, hence their collective name. The others have been discovered subsequently, some of them by the Voyager I probe. Jupiter's 6 outer moons orbit from east to west, the opposite direction of the inner moons.

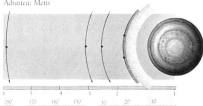

Inner moons (left to right): Io; Thebe; Almathea; Adrastea; Metis

Outer moons (left to right): Sinope; Pasiphae; Carme; Ananke; Elara; Lysithea; Himalia; Leda; Callisto; Ganymede; Europa; Io (also shown above)

SCALE IN RADIUSES OF JUPITER

JUPITER: SATELLITE DATA

	Diameter		Distance from Jupiter	
	miles	km	miles	km
Metis	27	43	79,500	128,000
Adrastea	10	16	80,200	129,000
Amalthea	104	167	112,500	181,000
Thebe	62	99	138,000	222,000
Io	2,264	3,643	262,000	422,000
Europa	1,941	3,124	417,000	671,000
Ganymede	3,722	5,265	665,000	1,070,000
Callisto	2,994	4,819	1,170,000	1,883,000
Leda	6	10	6,914,000	11,127,000
Himalia	106	170	7,133,000	11,480,000
Lysithea	15	24	7,261,000	11,686,000
Elara	50	80	7,293,000	11,737,000
Ananke	12	20	13,220,000	21,276,000
Carme	19	30	14,543,000	23,404,000
Pasiphae	22	36	14,679,000	23,624,000
Sinope	17	28	14,875,000	23,939,000

MORE FACTS

• The orbital periods of planetary satellites increase according to their distance from the planet. Innermost Metis orbits Jupiter in 0.295 Earth days, while Sinope takes 758 days.

• The Voyager probes obtained 30,000 images of Jupiter and its moons.

• The volcanoes on Io eject material at speeds up to 3,285 ft per sec (1,000 m/s). This is about 20 times faster than material from volcanoes on Earth.

SATURN

FAMED FOR ITS magnificent ring system, Saturn is the second largest of the planets. Like its nearest neighbor Jupiter, Saturn is a gas giant. However, the mass is so spread out that on average the planet is less dense than water. Titan is the largest of Saturn's 30 moons. It has a very thick atmosphere and is bigger than the planet Mercury.

RINGED WORLD
Saturn is at the limit of easy telescopic viewing from Earth. This photograph was taken at a distance of 11 million miles (17.5 million km) by Voyager 2.

Earth   *Saturn*

SATURN: PLANETARY DATA	
Average distance from the Sun:	886.7 million miles (1,427 million km)
Orbital period	29.45 Earth years
Orbital velocity	6 miles/sec (9.7 km/s)
Rotation period	10.23 hours
Diameter at equator	74,897 miles (120,536 km)
Cloud-top temperature	−292°F (−180°C)
Mass (Earth = 1)	95
Gravity (Earth = 1)	0.92
Number of moons	30

SATURN FACTS

• Saturn's rings are less than 656 ft (200 m) thick, but over 167,800 miles (270,000 km) in diameter.

• The rings consist of billions of ice-covered rock fragments and dust particles.

Ammonia
haze

Ammonia
clouds

Ammonium
hydrosulfide
clouds

Ice clouds

MUTED APPEARANCE
Saturn's atmosphere is
very similar to Jupiter's,
but it is colder. The cloud
layers are much thicker,
and have muted bands.

96% hydrogen

3% helium

Traces of methane,
ammonia, and water vapor

SATURN: ATMOSPHERE STRUCTURE AND COMPOSITION

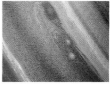

CYCLONIC STORM
False-color images show
cyclonic activity in Saturn's
atmosphere. The pale ovals
are rotating storms shaped
by powerful jet
streams.

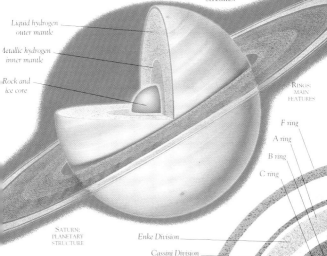

Liquid hydrogen
outer mantle

Metallic hydrogen
inner mantle

Rock and
ice core

RINGS:
MAIN
FEATURES

F ring

A ring

B ring

C ring

SATURN:
PLANETARY
STRUCTURE

Enke Division

Cassini Division

TILTED SYSTEM

Saturn rotates very rapidly on an axis
that is tilted at 26.7° to the vertical.
The orbits of the rings and moons are
all aligned with this rotation, and lie
in the same plane as the planet's
equator, giving the whole system a
tilted appearance. Like the other
giant gas planets, Saturn bulges
noticeably at the equator where
the speed of rotation is faster than
at the poles. Inside the atmosphere,
winds sweep around the equator at
1,120 mph (1,800 km/h).

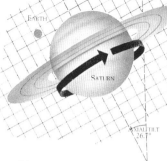

EARTH

SATURN

AXIAL TILT
26.7°

MANY MOONS

Saturn has 30 moons; one (Titan) is very
large, seven are of average size, and the
rest are small and irregularly shaped. Some
of the small moons are co-orbital: they
share an orbit with another moon. Mimas
(left), the closest of the larger moons, is
dominated by the huge crater Herschel,
perhaps the result of a co-orbital collision.

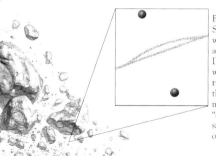

BRAIDED RINGS

Some of the inner moons orbit
within the rings, creating gaps
and braids. Pan sweeps the Encke
Division clear of ring material,
while Prometheus and Pandora
twist and braid the F ring with
their gravitational effect. These
moons are sometimes said to
"shepherd" the rings in the
same way that dogs keep a flock
of sheep together.

CROWDED SPACE

Saturn has both a pair and a triplet of co-orbital moons. In addition, two other moons, Janus and Epimetheus, have orbits that are extremely close to each other. Astronomers believe that these two were once a single moon that broke up.

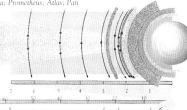

Inner moons (left to right): Helene and Dione (co-orbital); Calypso, Telesto, and Tethys (co-orbital); Enceladus; Mimas; Janus; Epimetheus; Pandora; Prometheus; Atlas; Pan

Outer moons (left to right): Phoebe; Iapetus; Hyperion; Titan; Rhea; Helene; and Dione (also shown above)

SCALE IN RADIUSES OF SATURN

SATURN: SATELLITE FACTS				
	Diameter		Distance from Saturn	
	miles	km	miles	km
Pan	12	20	83,000	133,580
Atlas	20	32	85,540	137,670
Prometheus	62	100	86,590	139,350
Pandora	52	84	88,050	141,700
Epimetheus	74	119	94,090	151,420
Janus	110	178	94,120	151,470
Mimas	247	397	115,280	185,520
Enceladus	310	499	147,900	238,020
Tethys	658	1,060	183,090	294,660
Telesto	14	22	183,090	294,660
Calypso	12	19	183,090	294,660
Dione	696	1,120	234,500	377,400
Helene	20	32	234,500	377,400
Rhea	949	1,528	327,490	527,040
Titan	3,200	5,150	759,210	1,221,830
Hyperion	165	266	920,310	1,481,100
Iapetus	892	1,436	2,212,900	3,561,300
Phoebe	137	220	8,048,000	12,952,000

MORE FACTS

• The rings of Saturn seem to be neatly graded, with the largest fragments found in the inner rings closest to the planet, while fine dust accumulates in the outer rings.

• Saturn is the only planet that has three moons sharing the same orbit – Tethys, Telesto, and Calypso.

• Mimas was to have been named "Arthur." Although this did not happen, many of its features are named after characters in the legend of King Arthur.

URANUS

A COLD GAS giant, Uranus is the seventh planet from the Sun. Little surface detail can be seen, and even close-up pictures show only a few clouds of frozen methane gas. Despite its featureless appearance, Uranus has one interesting peculiarity. The planet, and its rings and moons, are all tilted by more than 90°, traveling around the Sun on their side.

BLANK FACE
Faintly visible from Earth as a dim "star" in the night sky, Uranus was not identified as a planet until 1781. The ring system was not discovered until 1977 – almost 200 years later.

Earth

Uranus

URANUS: PLANETARY DATA	
Average distance from the Sun	1,784 million miles (2,871 million km)
Orbital period	84 Earth years
Orbital velocity	4.2 miles/sec (6.8 km/s)
Rotation period	17.24 hours
Diameter at equator	31,763 miles (51,118 km)
Cloud-top temperature	–346°F (–210°C)
Mass (Earth = 1)	14.5
Gravity (Earth = 1)	0.89
Number of moons	21

URANUS FACTS

• Uranus is named after Urania, the Greek muse (patron goddess) of astronomy.

• Light from the Sun, which takes about eight minutes to reach Earth, takes more than 2 hours 30 minutes to travel as far as Uranus.

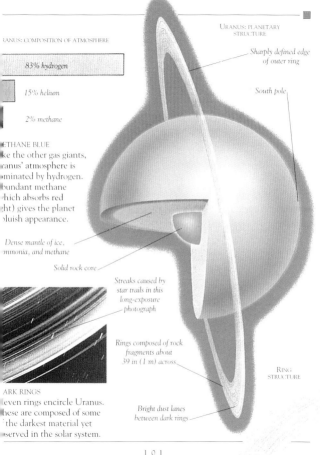

URANUS: COMPOSITION OF ATMOSPHERE

83% hydrogen

15% helium

2% methane

Sharply defined edge
of outer ring

South pole

ETHANE BLUE
Like the other gas giants,
Uranus' atmosphere is
dominated by hydrogen.
Abundant methane
which absorbs red
light) gives the planet
a bluish appearance.

Dense mantle of ice,
ammonia, and methane

Solid rock core

Streaks caused by
star trails in this
long-exposure
photograph

Rings composed of rock
fragments about
39 in (1 m) across

RING
STRUCTURE

DARK RINGS
Eleven rings encircle Uranus.
These are composed of some
of the darkest material yet
observed in the solar system.

Bright dust lanes
between dark rings

SIDEWAYS ORBIT

Uranus' axis of rotation is tilted at 98° to the vertical – the equator runs through the "top" and "bottom" of the planet. This extreme tilt also extends to the rings and moons. Uranus' sideways stance may have been the result of a collision with another celestial body at some time in the distant past.

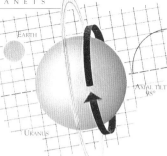

EARTH

AXIAL TILT 98°

URANUS

LENGTHY SEASONS

Uranus' peculiar tilt creates extremely long seasons. As the planet travels around the Sun, each pole receives 42 Earth years of sunlight, followed by the same period of total darkness. However, the temperature does not vary with the seasons because Uranus is so far away from the Sun.

STRANGE MAGNETISM

Uranus generates a magnetic field which is tilted, but not the same way as the planet. The magnetic field is tilted at 60° to the axis of rotation, which means that the magnetosphere has a fairly normal shape. To make the situation even more extraordinary, Uranus' magnetic field is offset from the planet's center.

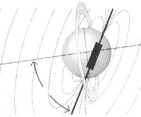

RINGS AND MOONS
Only the innermost moon, Cordelia, orbits within the ring system. Miranda is perhaps the most unusual moon in the solar system – it shows every sign of once having been blasted apart and then reassembled.

Inner moons (left to right): Puck; Belinda; Rosalind; Portia; Juliet; Desdemona; Cressida; Bianca; Ophelia; Cordelia

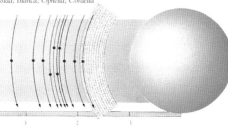

Outer moons (left to right): Oberon; Titania; Umbriel; Ariel; Miranda; Puck (also shown above)

URANUS: SATELLITE DATA				
	Diameter		Distance from Uranus	
	miles	km	miles	km
Bianca	26	42	36,770	59,170
Cressida	39	62	38,390	61,780
Desdemona	34	54	38,950	62,680
Juliet	52	84	39,990	64,350
Portia	67	108	41,070	66,090
Rosalind	34	54	43,460	69,940
Belinda	41	66	46,760	75,260
Puck	96	154	53,440	86,010
Miranda	293	472	80,400	129,390
Ariel	719	1,158	118,690	191,020
Umbriel	727	1,169	165,470	266,300
Titania	980	1,578	270,860	435,910
Oberon	946	1,523	362,580	583,520
Caliban	37	60	4,455,500	7,170,400
Sycorax	75	120	7,590,700	12,216,000

MORE FACTS
• Before Voyager 2, Uranus was believed to have five moons. The accepted total is now 21, with more awaiting confirmation.

• Many of the Uranian moons are named after characters in plays by William Shakespeare.

• In contrast to the planet Saturn, the outermost Uranian ring has no fragments less than about 8 in (20 cm) across.

NEPTUNE

THE OUTERMOST of the gas giants, Neptune is a near twin to Uranus. Too faint to be seen easily from Earth, its position was calculated mathematically. Neptune was first observed in 1846 exactly where it was predicted to be. Methane in the atmosphere gives Neptune a deep blue coloration. The rings and six of the moons were discovered by the Voyager 2 probe.

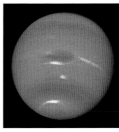

DARK STORMS
In this photograph, by the Voyager 2 probe in 1989, Neptune shows a huge cyclonic storm, called the Great Dark Spot (center right), overlain by bright, wispy methane clouds.

Earth

Neptune

NEPTUNE: PLANETARY DATA	
Average distance from the Sun	2,795 million miles (4,498 million km)
Orbital period	164.8 Earth years
Orbital velocity	3.4 miles/sec (5.4 km/s)
Rotation period	16.11 hours
Diameter at equator	30,775 miles (49,528 km)
Cloud-top temperature	−364°F (−220°C)
Mass (Earth = 1)	17.1
Gravity (Earth = 1)	1.1
Number of moons	11

NEPTUNE FACTS
• Neptune is named after the Roman god of the sea.
• Neptune radiates 2.6 times more heat than it receives from the Sun – a sign of an internal source of heat.

NEPTUNE: COMPOSITION OF ATMOSPHERE

80% hydrogen

19% helium

1% methane

HYDROCARBON HAZE

Otherwise very similar to that of Uranus, Neptune's atmosphere has a deeper blue color. The highest level contains a thin hydrocarbon haze.

CIRRUS CLOUDS

High-altitude cirrus clouds of frozen methane crystals. These clouds are situated about 25 miles (40 km) above the main cloud layer.

Methane, ammonia, and ice mantle

Silicate rock core

Adam's ring

Le Verrier ring

Galle ring

Great Dark Spot

Dark low-altitude clouds of hydrogen sulfide

Lassell ring

NEPTUNE: PLANETARY STRUCTURE

RING STRUCTURE

LACK OF SEASONS

Neptune rotates on its axis at approximately the same angle of tilt as Earth. However, Neptune is far too distant from the Sun for the tilt to result in a similar cycle of seasons. Conditions in the atmosphere are dominated by winds blowing at up to 1,250 mph (2,000 km/s) which carry the dark storms around the planet in a backward direction.

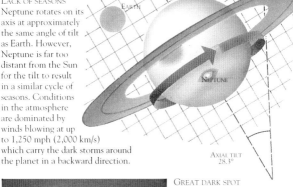

EARTH

NEPTUNE

AXIAL TILT
28.3°

GREAT DARK SPOT

Neptune's largest storm, the Great Dark Spot, is about the same size as Earth and rotates in a counter-clockwise direction. The bright spot below it is a cloud called the Scooter, which travels around the planet faster than the Great Dark Spot.

TRITON

The largest of Neptune's moons, Triton is the coldest place in the solar system at –391°F (–235°C). It has a thin atmosphere, mainly of nitrogen, and a large south polar ice cap composed of methane ice. Photographs show the ice to have a pink tinge, which is believed to be due to the presence of organic chemicals formed by the action of sunlight.

Inner moons (left to right): Larissa; Galatea; Despina; Thalassa; Naiad

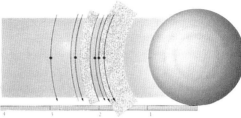

CIRCLING NEPTUNE

The four innermost moons orbit within the ring system. Triton is the only large moon in the solar system that orbits in a backward direction compared to the planet's rotation.

SCALE IN RADIUSES OF NEPTUNE

Outer moons (left to right): Nereid; Triton; Proteus; Larissa; and inner moons (also shown above)

DISTANT EXPLORER

Voyager 2 is the only probe that has so far visited Uranus and Neptune. The journey to Neptune took 12 years, and information from Voyager 2 (transmitted at the speed of light) took more than four hours to reach Earth. Among Voyager 2's many discoveries were six of Neptune's eight moons and ice volcanoes on Triton.

VOYAGER 2

NEPTUNE: SATELLITE DATA				
	Diameter		Distance from Neptune	
	miles	km	miles	km
Naiad	36	58	29,970	48,230
Thalassa	50	80	31,110	50,070
Despina	92	148	32,640	52,530
Galatea	98	158	38,490	61,950
Larissa	119	192	45,700	73,550
Proteus	258	416	73,100	117,650
Triton	1,681	2,705	220,440	354,760
Nereid	211	340	3,425,900	5,513,400

FACT

• The outermost moon, Nereid, has the most eccentric orbit of any known satellite. During a single orbit, Nereid's distance from Neptune varies between 800,000 miles (1,300,000 km) and 6,000,000 miles (9,700,000 km).

PLUTO

THE MOST DISTANT of all the planets, Pluto, is also the least understood. Pluto's orbit around the Sun is uniquely tilted at 17°, and is highly unusual in other ways. For about ten percent of its long orbital path, Pluto is closer to the Sun than Neptune. Pluto has a single large moon, Charon, and together they form a double planet.

BLURRED IMAGE
The clearest image of Pluto and Charon has been obtained by the Hubble Space Telescope orbiting Earth. Ground-based photographs show a single blur.

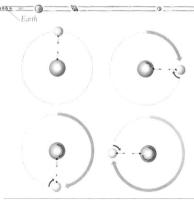

Earth   Pluto

CLOSELY LINKED SYSTEM
Pluto and Charon exhibit a powerful effect on each other. Charon's orbit around Pluto has become synchronized with Pluto's own rotation, so that both have the same period – 6.4 Earth days. As a result, the same face of Charon is always turned to the same face of Pluto. From one side of Pluto, Charon is always visible in the sky. From the other side of the planet, the moon cannot be seen at all.

PLUTO: PLANETARY DATA

Average distance from the Sun	3,670 million miles (5,906.4 million km)
Orbital period	247.9 Earth years
Orbital velocity	2.9 miles/sec (4.7 kms)
Rotation period	6.38 Earth days
Diameter at equator	1,485 miles (2,390 km)
Surface temperature	–382°F (–230°C)
Mass (Earth = 1)	0.06
Gravity (Earth = 1)	0.04 Moons: 1

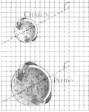

EXTREME TILT
Pluto and Charon both
rotate on axes that are
tilted at 122.6° to the
vertical – the least
upright of all the
planets.

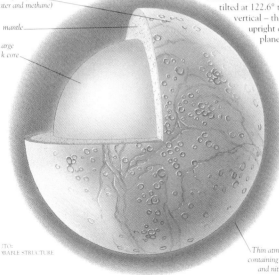

Icy surface
(water and methane)

mantle

Large
dark core

PLUTO:
PROBABLE STRUCTURE

Thin atmosphere
containing methane
and nitrogen

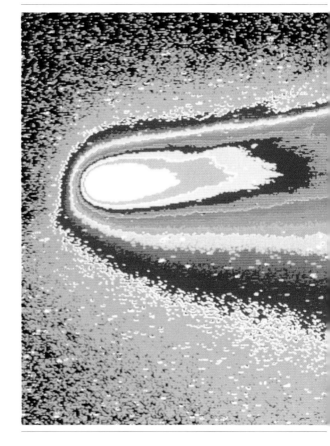

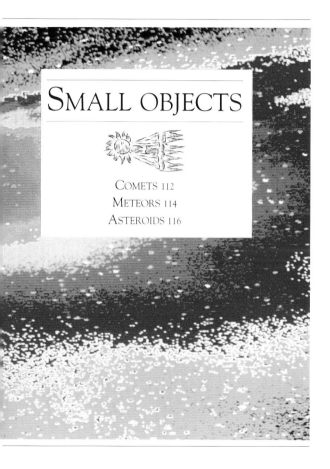

SMALL OBJECTS

COMETS

A COMET IS a "dirty snowball" composed of snow and dust. Billions of comets orbit the Sun at a distance of about one light-year. A few comets have orbits that take them closer to the Sun. As they near the Sun and are heated, the snow turns to gas and forms a long bright tail.

COMET HALLEY
Most comets that approach the Sun are seen only once, but a few return periodically. Comet Halley returns every 76 years.

ORBITING THE SUN
A periodic comet has a regular orbit that brings it close to the Sun. For most of its orbit, the comet has no tail. The tail only develops as the comet nears the Sun and its surface is heated. The tail gets longer and longer, and then disappears as the comet moves away from the Sun.

Tail develops as the comet approaches the Sun

SUN

Tail is longest near the Sun

For most of its orbit, a comet is a tailless dirty snowball.

Tail shrinks as comet moves away

GLOWING GAS

The nucleus of a typical comet
is about 0.62 miles (1 km)
across. When heated by the
Sun, jets of gas and dust
erupt from the surface of
the nucleus to form a
glowing cloud called a
coma, which surrounds
the nucleus. The coma
can be 10 times larger
than the Earth. The
comet's tail may be
millions of miles
(kilometers) long.

*Comets often have two
distinct tails, one of
gas and one of dust.*

Coma

Nucleus made of dust
and frozen gases

Dust reflects sunlight

HEART OF A COMET

This photograph of the nucleus of Comet
Halley was taken by the Giotto probe from a
distance of about 1,050 miles (1,700 km).
Bright gas jets can be seen on the sunlit
(upper) surface. Instruments aboard Giotto
showed that the main constituent of the
nucleus was water-ice.

COMET FACT

• The planet Jupiter is
so large that its gravity
can affect the orbit
of comets. In 1992,
Comet Shoemaker-
Levy passed close to
Jupiter and was broken
into several fragments
by gravitational forces.
During July 1994, these
fragments crashed
into Jupiter, causing
a series of huge
explosions in Jupiter's
atmosphere.

METEORS

EVERY DAY, thousands of dust particles and rock fragments from space enter the Earth's atmosphere. Most burn up due to friction with the air. The streaks of light they produce are called meteors. Very rarely a larger fragment survives the atmosphere and hits Earth's surface. These "space-rocks" are called meteorites.

METEOR SHOWER
This is a a false-color photograph of a Leonid meteor shower (yellow streaks), which is associated with Comet Tempel-Tuttle.

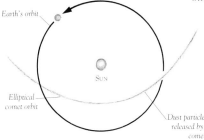

Earth's orbit

SUN

Elliptical comet orbit

Dust particles released by comet

CROSSING ORBITS
Most meteors are caused by dust and debris shed by comets as they pass close to the Sun. The debris stays in the path of the comet's orbit; and when the Earth's orbit crosses that of the comet, we experience a meteor shower. Some showers are regular annual events.

METEOR FACTS

• Each year 48,400 tons (44,000 tonnes) of extra-terrestrial material enters our atmosphere.

• Most meteors are vaporized at altitudes above 50 miles (80 km).

• Meteor showers are named after the constellation in which the radiant appears, e.g. the Perseids.

• In very heavy storms, thousands of meteors fall each hour.

STONY
METEORITE

Fragments of
nickel-iron embedded
in a matrix of rock

Heat-blackened
surface

STONY-IRON
METEORITE

STONES AND IRONS FROM SPACE
There are two main types of meteorite – those
composed mainly of rock (called "stones") and
those made mostly of metal (called "irons").
Rocky meteorites are far more common than
"irons," but the rarest meteorites on Earth (less
than one in every hundred found) are "stony-
irons" that contain both metal and rock.

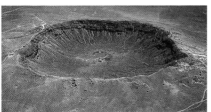

IMPACT CRATER
Barringer Crater in Arizona measures 0.8 miles
(1.3 km) across. It was formed about 50,000
years ago when a meteorite about 150 ft (45 m)
in diameter struck the surface at a speed of
around 6.8 miles/sec (11 km/s). Meteorite
hunters have found several "iron" fragments
in the crater.

METEORITE FACTS
• More than 90% of
identified meteorites
that strike the Earth
are "stones."

• The world's largest
known meteorite still
lies where it fell at
Hoba West in southern
Africa. Its weight is
estimated at over 60
tons (tonnes).

• Last century, Czar
Alexander of Russia
had a sword made from
an "iron" meteorite.

ASTEROIDS

MILLIONS OF CHUNKS of rock
orbit the Sun. These are the
asteroids, sometimes called
the minor planets. Asteroids
range in size from a few feet
(meters) across, to those that
are hundreds of miles
(kilometers) in diameter.
Most of the asteroids are
found in a wide belt between
the orbits of Mars and Jupiter.

SPACE ROCK
Ida is a typical asteroid – small
and irregular in shape with a
maximum length of 34 miles
(55 km). Its surface is heavily
cratered and covered by a thin
layer of dust.

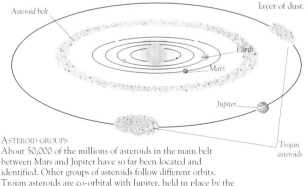

Asteroid belt

Earth

Mars

Jupiter

Trojan
asteroids

ASTEROID GROUPS
About 50,000 of the millions of asteroids in the main belt
between Mars and Jupiter have so far been located and
identified. Other groups of asteroids follow different orbits.
Trojan asteroids are co-orbital with Jupiter, held in place by the
giant planet's powerful gravity.

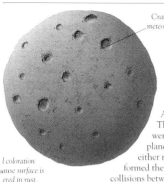

*Craters due to
meteorite impacts*

*Most asteroids are
irregular in shape.*

*l coloration
ause surface is
ered in rust*

ASTEROID ORIGINS

The larger asteroids are spherical and
were formed in the same way as the
planets. The smaller irregular asteroids are
either remnants of the original material that
formed the solar system, or the result of
collisions between two or more large asteroids.

FAILED PLANET

The asteroid belt was probably
formed at the same time as the rest
of the solar system. Rock fragments
and dust particles in this part of the
system were prevented from
clumping together to form a
planet by Jupiter's gravity.
But if all the asteroids were
put together, their mass
would be only a tiny
fraction of
the Earth's.

ASTEROID FACTS

• The first asteroid to
e discovered was Ceres
which has a diameter of
84 miles (940 km).

• Asteroids which have
n average distance
com the Sun less than
arth's are known as
Aten asteroids.

• Earth has been struck
y several asteroids in
he past, and it is only a
aatter of time before
nother asteroid strikes
ur planet.

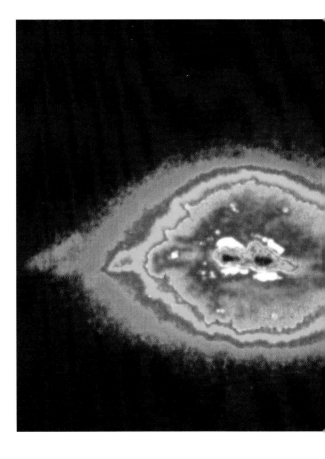

STUDYING SPACE

INFORMATION FROM SPACE

GATHERING AND STUDYING starlight is just one way that we learn about the universe. Visible light is only a small part of the electromagnetic spectrum, which covers all forms of radiation. By studying different types of radiation, we learn more about both the visible and the invisible parts of the universe.

Ozone layer

Gamma rays and X-rays

UV rays

Most infrared stopped here

Visible light and short-wave radio reach surface

ATMOSPHERIC SHIELD
The atmosphere shields Earth against radiation from space. Gamma rays, X-rays, and most ultraviolet (UV) rays are stopped. Only visible light, some infrared and UV radiation, and some radio signals reach the surface.

INFORMATION SPECTRUM
Electromagnetic radiation travels through space as waves of varying length (the distance between wave crests). Gamma rays have the shortest wavelength, then X-rays, and so on through the spectrum to the longest radio waves. Visible light, which is all that we can see naturally, occupies a very narrow portion (less than 0.00001 percent) of the spectrum.

10^{-11} m
0.00000000000001 meters

X-RAYS

GAMMA RAYS

CRAB NEBULA AT DIFFERENT WAVELENGTHS

The Crab Nebula – the remnant of a supernova explosion seen in 1054 – emits a wide range of radiation wavelengths. When viewed in infrared light (right) the nebula looks like a huge cloud. The red areas represent the cooler parts of the nebula.

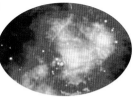

VISIBLE LIGHT

In visible light, vast filaments of hot gas can be seen spreading out into space after the explosion. The blue glow comes from fast-moving particles accelerated by the strong magnetic field of the inner nebula.

X-RAY

An X-ray image (right) reveals the source of the magnetism – a rapidly spinning pulsar at the heart of the nebula. The pulsar is surrounded by high-energy particles that spiral around the pulsar's magnetic field lines.

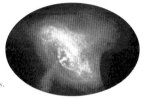

10^{-7} m
0.0000001 meters

10^{5} m
100,000 meters

VISIBLE
LIGHT

MICROWAVES

RAVIOLET
.IGHT

INFRARED
LIGHT

RADIO
WAVES

OPTICAL TELESCOPES

THE OPTICAL TELESCOPE is one of the main tools of astronomy. But little time is spent looking through a telescope eyepiece – modern instruments collect and store visual information electronically. The optical telescope remains an important tool because it gathers basic information.

PALOMAR DOME
The protective dome of the Hale Telescope at the Mount Palomar Observatory, California, shields the telescope from the effects of weather.

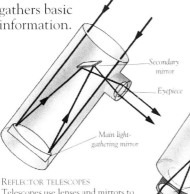

Secondary mirror

Eyepiece

Main light-gathering mirror

Main light-gathering lens

Eyepiece lens

REFLECTOR TELESCOPES
Telescopes use lenses and mirrors to gather light and produce an image. Reflector telescopes, which make use of curved mirrors, are the most useful type for astronomy.

REFRACTOR TELESCOPES
Refractor telescopes use only lense They cannot be made in such large sizes as reflector telescopes, but they remain very popular with amateur astronomers.

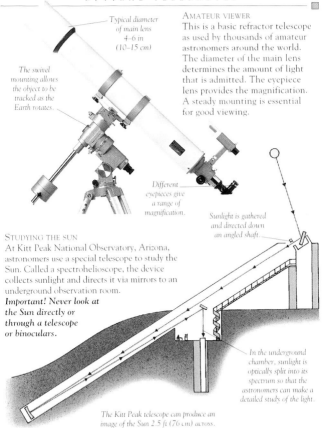

Typical diameter
of main lens
4–6 in
(10–15 cm)

The swivel
mounting allows
the object to be
tracked as the
Earth rotates.

Different
eyepieces give
a range of
magnification.

AMATEUR VIEWER
This is a basic refractor telescope
as used by thousands of amateur
astronomers around the world.
The diameter of the main lens
determines the amount of light
that is admitted. The eyepiece
lens provides the magnification.
A steady mounting is essential
for good viewing.

Sunlight is gathered
and directed down
an angled shaft.

STUDYING THE SUN
At Kitt Peak National Observatory, Arizona,
astronomers use a special telescope to study the
Sun. Called a spectrohelioscope, the device
collects sunlight and directs it via mirrors to an
underground observation room.
**Important! Never look at
the Sun directly or
through a telescope
or binoculars.**

In the underground
chamber, sunlight is
optically split into its
spectrum so that the
astronomers can make a
detailed study of the light.

The Kitt Peak telescope can produce an
image of the Sun 2.5 ft (76 cm) across.

RADIO ASTRONOMY

WE HAVE BEEN LISTENING in to the radio energy of the universe for more than 50 years. Radio astronomy can obtain additional information about familiar objects, as well as seek out new ones. Two major discoveries – quasars and pulsars – were made by radio astronomers.

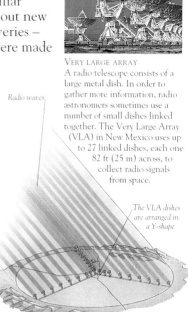

VERY LARGE ARRAY
A radio telescope consists of a large metal dish. In order to gather more information, radio astronomers sometimes use a number of small dishes linked together. The Very Large Array (VLA) in New Mexico uses up to 27 linked dishes, each one 82 ft (25 m) across, to collect radio signals from space.

Radio waves

The VLA dishes are arranged in a Y-shape

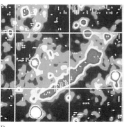

RADIO VISION
Radio telescopes, like ordinary radio sets, can be tuned to a particular wavelength, and the intensity of the radio energy can be measured. Computers are then used to produce "radio-maps" of the sky, such as this image of the bar-shaped radio source known as 1952+28.

LARGEST DISH

The world's largest radio telescope, the 1,000 ft (305 m) Arecibo dish, is built into a natural hollow in the hills of Puerto Rico. The dish is "steered" using the Earth's own rotation. Arecibo has also been used to send a radio message out into space.

Simple processing of the Arecibo message produces this visual image which contains a representation of a human being.

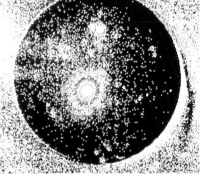

RADIO GALAXIES

Many galaxies that are quite faint visually are very "bright" at radio wavelengths. These are often called radio galaxies, or active galaxies. This optical image of radio galaxy 3C 33 has been color-coded according to the intensity of light in the visible part of the spectrum ranging from white (most intense) to blue (the least).

IMAGES OF SPACE

MUCH OF THE information that astronomers obtain through their instruments is presented as visual images. Conventional and electronic cameras are used to record these images. The information is usually stored on computers that can process images to improve the picture and bring out details.

PIXELATED VIEW
Electronic cameras make image with a grid of tiny picture-elements (pixels). This view of dim and distant star cluster was obtained with a ground-based telescope. The individual pixel are clearly visible, although it takes a trained eye to identify t image as a star cluster.

MARTIAN CHEMICAL PHOTOMAP
This image of the Martian surface was produced from data collected by a device called a neutron spectrometer aboard the Mars Odyssey probe. It is color-coded to show concentrations of hydrogen in the soil. Deep blue areas contain the most hydrogen, and red areas the least. In the deep blue regions near the poles, the hydrogen is mostly combined with oxygen in the form of water ice.

Soil near the poles may be up to 50 percent water ice.

FALSE COLOR GIVES A TRUER VIEW
Astronomers have several techniques for
analyzing the information contained in
images. One of the most important is
adding false color to the image.
Saturn has a fairly muted appearance
in ordinary photographs. This
image has been color-coded to
emphasize the banding of
the planet's upper
atmosphere.

COLORING THE SUN
This false-color ultraviolet image
from the TRACE spacecraft shows
plasma exploding off the Sun's
surface and traveling through the
solar atmosphere along loops of the
Sun's magnetic field. The colors
represent different temperatures.
The red regions are the hottest,
at 2.7 milllion°F (1.5 million°C).

SEPARATE, THEN COMBINE
Images of space are often obtained through a series
of colored filters. The object is photographed
through each filter in turn, and the resulting
images are then combined to give a much fuller
picture than with any single ordinary photograph.
This series was taken with the Hubble Space
Telescope, and shows Pluto and its moon Charon.

OBSERVATORIES

OPTICAL TELESCOPES are usually installed in mountain-top observatories, where they suffer the least interference from Earth's atmosphere. Radio telescopes can be situated almost anywhere, and are usually located near universities. Observatories are often shared between countries because of the high cost of telescopes which use the latest technology.

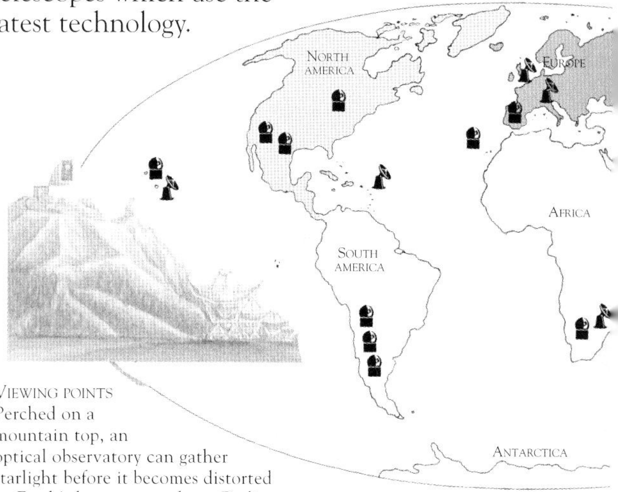

NORTH AMERICA

EUROPE

AFRICA

SOUTH AMERICA

ANTARCTICA

VIEWING POINTS
Perched on a mountain top, an optical observatory can gather starlight before it becomes distorted by Earth's lower atmosphere. Radio telescopes are unaffected by altitude and are built where convenient.

HIGH AND DRY

The European Southern Observatory is sited on Cerro Paranal, a 8,645-ft- (2,635-m-) high mountain in Chile's Atacama desert. A dry climate with cloud-free nights and a steady atmosphere makes this remote location ideal for clear viewing.

AUSTRALASIA

MAP KEY

OPTICAL TELESCOPE

RADIO TELESCOPE

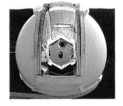

HIGH-TECH TELESCOPE

The Keck Telescope situated on Mauna Kea, Hawaii, is the world's largest optical telescope. The main mirror is made up of 36 computer-controlled hexagonal segments.

TELESCOPES IN SPACE

BY PLACING THEIR TELESCOPES in
orbit above Earth's atmosphere,
astronomers get a much better
view. They can see farther and
can collect information from
wavelengths that are absorbed
by the atmosphere. Information
and images gathered in orbit
are transmitted back to Earth
for study and analysis.

ORBITING TELESCOPE
Two astronauts from the
Space Shuttle *Columbia*
make repairs to the Hubble
Space Telescope in 2002.

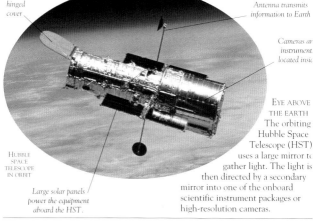

*Protective
hinged
cover*

*Antenna transmits
information to Earth*

Cameras an
instrument
located insi

EYE ABOVE
THE EARTH
The orbiting
Hubble Space
Telescope (HST)
uses a large mirror to
gather light. The light is
then directed by a secondary
mirror into one of the onboard
scientific instrument packages or
high-resolution cameras.

HUBBLE
SPACE
TELESCOPE
IN ORBIT

*Large solar panels
power the equipment
aboard the HST.*

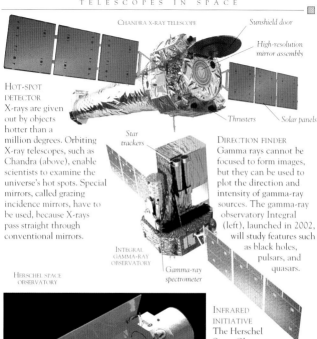

CHANDRA X-RAY TELESCOPE

Sunshield door

High-resolution mirror assembly

HOT-SPOT
DETECTOR
X-rays are given
out by objects
hotter than a
million degrees. Orbiting
X-ray telescopes, such as
Chandra (above), enable
scientists to examine the
universe's hot spots. Special
mirrors, called grazing
incidence mirrors, have to
be used, because X-rays
pass straight through
conventional mirrors.

Thrusters

Solar panels

Star trackers

DIRECTION FINDER
Gamma rays cannot be
focused to form images,
but they can be used to
plot the direction and
intensity of gamma-ray
sources. The gamma-ray
observatory Integral
(left), launched in 2002,
will study features such
as black holes,
pulsars, and
quasars.

INTEGRAL
GAMMA-RAY
OBSERVATORY

Gamma-ray spectrometer

HERSCHEL SPACE
OBSERVATORY

INFRARED
INITIATIVE
The Herschel
Space Observatory,
an orbiting infrared
telescope to be launched
in 2007, will study the
universe at infrared
wavelengths not covered
before. One of its tasks
will be to investigate how
stars and galaxies form.

ROCKETS

SATELLITES, SPACE PROBES, and astronauts are lifted into space by rockets. There are two main types. The conventional tall, thin rocket is made from several stages stacked on top of each other. The newer Space Shuttle design lifts off with the aid of massive booster rockets. But when it returns from space, the Shuttle lands like an aircraft.

LIFTOFF
A Soyuz-Fregat rocket blasts off from the launchpad. Its engines burn fuel at a rate of thousands of gallons (liters) per second.

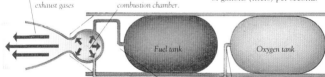

Nozzle shapes the stream of hot exhaust gases

Liquid fuel and oxygen are combined in the combustion chamber.

Fuel tank

Oxygen tank

Fuel and oxygen stored in reinforced pressurised tanks

Pumps control the flow of fuel and oxygen to the combustion chamber.

ROCKET POWER
A rocket is propelled upward by hot exhaust gases streaming from nozzles at the tail. These gases are the result of burning a mixture of liquid oxygen and fuel (such as liquid hydrogen) inside a combustion chamber. Carrying its own oxygen supply enables a rocket engine to function in the airless vacuum of space.

Payload –
satellite or
space probe

ESCAPE VELOCITY

A rocket, or any other object, is held on the Earth's surface by the force of gravity. To escape the effects of Earth's gravity and enter space, a rocket needs to achieve a speed of 24,840 mph (40,000 km/h) – this is the "escape velocity" of planet Earth. On the Moon, where the force of gravity is only one sixth as powerful as on Earth, the escape velocity is lower – only about 5,300 mph (8,500 km/h).

Third-stage rocket engines

ARIANE: A TYPICAL
THREE-STAGE LAUNCH VEHICLE

Second-stage rocket engines

First-stage rocket engines

External booster rockets assist first stage engines at liftoff

REUSABLE SPACE CRAFT

streaming exhaust trail marks the beginning another Space Shuttle mission. Unlike onventional rockets, which can be used only nce, the Shuttle is reusable. The massive ooster rockets are jettisoned two minutes after aunch and recovered. The Shuttle's own ngines carry it on into orbit, and small thruster ockets are used to maneuver it into position.

FLYBYS AND ORBITERS

LIFTED INTO SPACE by rockets, space probes are computer-controlled robots packed with scientific instruments. Probes are sent to fly by a planet, or even orbit around it, sending data and images back to Earth. After they have completed their planned missions, some probes continue on into space.

VOLCANIC DISCOVERY
The probe Voyager 1 obtained this image of Io which shows the first active volcano seen outside Earth.

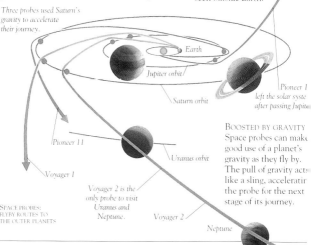

Three probes used Saturn's gravity to accelerate their journey.

Earth

Jupiter orbit

Saturn orbit

Pioneer 1 left the solar system after passing Jupiter.

Pioneer 11

Uranus orbit

Voyager 1

Voyager 2 is the only probe to visit Uranus and Neptune.

Voyager 2

Neptune

BOOSTED BY GRAVITY
Space probes can make good use of a planet's gravity as they fly by. The pull of gravity acts like a sling, accelerating the probe for the next stage of its journey.

SPACE PROBES:
FLYBY ROUTES TO
THE OUTER PLANETS

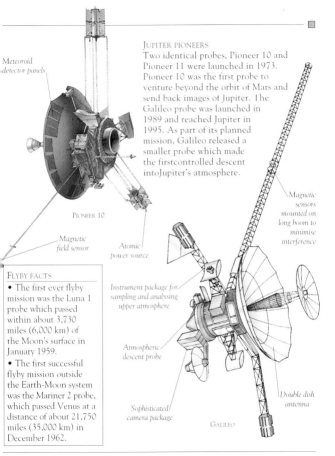

JUPITER PIONEERS

Two identical probes, Pioneer 10 and
Pioneer 11 were launched in 1973.
Pioneer 10 was the first probe to
venture beyond the orbit of Mars and
send back images of Jupiter. The
Galileo probe was launched in
1989 and reached Jupiter in
1995. As part of its planned
mission, Galileo released a
smaller probe which made
the first controlled descent
into Jupiter's atmosphere.

Meteoroid
detector panels

PIONEER 10

Magnetic
field sensor

Atomic
power source

Magnetic
sensors
mounted on
long boom to
minimise
interference

Instrument package for
sampling and analysing
upper atmosphere

Atmospheric
descent probe

Double dish
antenna

Sophisticated
camera package

GALILEO

LANDERS

SPACE PROBES SENT to orbit a
planet can release a second
craft to land on the surface.
The lander, a scientific robot,
carries out its preprogrammed
tasks and then relays the data
it has obtained back to Earth.
Only six piloted spacecraft
have made landings, during
the Apollo Moon program.

IS THERE LIFE ON MARS?

Two Viking orbiter craft each
released a lander that descended
safely to the Martian surface. In total
about 3,000 photographic images
were sent back to Earth. The landers
also tested the Martian soil with four
different experiments to check for
any signs of life – none
was found.

COMING IN TO LAND
This dramatic photograph of
the Hadley Rille valley was
taken from the piloted Apollo
15 lander during its low-altitude
descent to the Moon's surface.

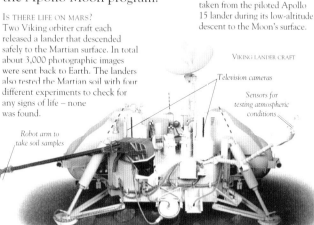

VIKING LANDER CRAFT

Television cameras

Sensors for
testing atmospheric
conditions

Robot arm to
take soil samples

The two parts separate
and the lander
begins its descent
through the atmosphere.

The protective
atmospheric shield
is jettisoned

VENERA 9 LANDER CRAFT

On-board braking
engines begin to slow
Venera 9

LANDER FACTS

• The first successful
lander was Luna 9,
which soft-landed on
the Moon in 1966.

• Venera 7 became the
first lander to transmit
data from the surface of
Venus in 1970.

• The Viking landers
analysed Mars' soil and
found that it contained
the following chemical
elements:

silica	14%
iron	18%
aluminum	2.7%
titanium	0.9%
potassium	0.3%

HOT LANDING

A series of Venera space
probes was sent to Venus.
Each consisted of two parts,
one of which descended to
the surface. Conditions on
Venus – very high temperature
and pressure – meant that
the landers could function
only for a few minutes.

Parachutes
further slow the
descent

Venera 9 obtains
and transmits
several images
before failing

WORKING IN SPACE

ASTRONAUTS NOW WORK in space on a regular basis. Many experiments take place aboard orbiting laboratories, while satellites can be launched, retrieved, and repaired while circling Earth.

WORKING ON THE MOON
Buzz Aldrin (the second person to walk on the Moon) sets up one of the scientific experiment packages that the Apollo 11 crew left behind on the lunar surface.

Antenna

Television camera

Steering control

Equipment storage rack

Wire-mesh wheels

LUNAR ROVING VEHICLE (LRV)

MOON BUGGY
Crew members of the Apollo 15, 16, and 17 missions made effective use of the LRV. This "moon-buggy" enabled them to travel dozens of miles across the lunar surface, collecting samples over a wide area.

SPACE SCIENCE
Orbiting laboratories allow scientists to carry out experiments in conditions where gravity's influence is negligible. This scientist is testing how fuel burns in a weightless enironment.

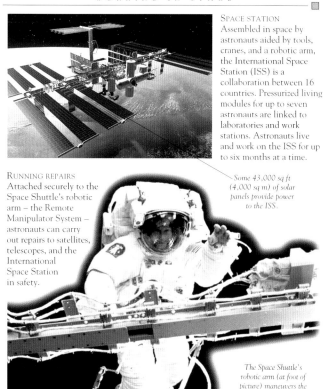

SPACE STATION
Assembled in space by astronauts aided by tools, cranes, and a robotic arm, the International Space Station (ISS) is a collaboration between 16 countries. Pressurized living modules for up to seven astronauts are linked to laboratories and work stations. Astronauts live and work on the ISS for up to six months at a time.

Some 43,000 sq ft (4,000 sq m) of solar panels provide power to the ISS.

RUNNING REPAIRS
Attached securely to the Space Shuttle's robotic arm – the Remote Manipulator System – astronauts can carry out repairs to satellites, telescopes, and the International Space Station in safety.

The Space Shuttle's robotic arm (at foot of picture) maneuvers the astronaut into the correct position to carry out a particular task.

SPACE HISTORY

MILESTONES IN ASTRONOMY

The astronomer's job is to observe, describe, and explain objects in space. The story of astronomy is marked by a series of milestone achievements. Advances in technology have led to better descriptions and more comprehensive explanations.

EUDOXUS OF CNIDUS (408-355 B.C.) was a Greek thinker who studied at Athens under the philosopher Plato. In later life he developed the theory of crystal spheres – the first scientific attempt to explain the observed motion of the planets, and stars.

MILESTONE
According to Eudoxus, the Earth was at the center of the universe. The stars and planets were set into a series of transparent crystal spheres that surrounded the Earth in space.

PTOLEMY (c.A.D. 120-180) lived in Alexandria, Egypt, at the height of the Roman Empire. Although little is known about him, he has become famous as the "father of astronomy." The idea that the Earth is at the center of the universe is often referred to as the "Ptolemaic System."

MILESTONE
He compiled a compendium, known as the "Almagest," of ancient Greek astronomical knowledge. Handed down over the centuries, Ptolemy's book continued to provide the basis of scientific astronomy for more than 1,000 years.

AL-SUFI (903-86) was a Persian nobleman, and one of the leading astronomers of his time. His "Book of Fixed Stars" listed the position and brightness of more than 1,000 stars, and beautifully illustrated the main constellations.

MILESTONE
During the Dark Ages, scientific astronomy was kept alive in the Islamic empire. Our knowledge of the works of Ptolemy is entirely due to Arab translators.

NICOLAUS COPERNICUS (1473-1543) worked as a church lawyer in Poland. Near the end of his life he published an exciting new view of the universe which replaced Ptolemy's.

MILESTONE
Copernicus removed the Earth from its traditional place at the center of the universe, and replaced it with the Sun. This was considered to be revolutionary view, and the "Copernican Revolution" was strongly opposed by the Christian Church.

GALILEO GALILEI (1564-1642) was an Italian scientist and astronomer who supported Copernicus' new theory. As a result, he was put on trial by the Church, and he remained a virtual prisoner for the rest of his life.

MILESTONE
Galileo pioneered the use of the refractor telescope for astronomy. He made several major discoveries, including mountains on the Moon, the phases of Venus, and the four largest moons of Jupiter.

ISAAC NEWTON (1643-1727) was a professor of mathematics and a great scientist. He is supposed to have had the idea for his theory of gravity after seeing an apple fall from a tree.

MILESTONE
The theory of gravity explained why apples fall, and why planets orbit around the Sun. Newton was able to establish the scientific laws that apply to the motion of objects in space. He also experimented with optics – splitting sunlight into its spectrum – and designed a reflecting telescope.

EDMOND HALLEY (1656-1742) became Britain's Astronomer Royal – one of the first official government scientists. As a young man he voyaged to the remote island of St. Helena, and charted the stars of the Southern Hemisphere.

MILESTONE
Halley is famous for predicting the return of the periodic comet that now bears his name. His work reinforced the idea that astronomy is a very precise science that can make accurate predictions.

WILLIAM HERSCHEL (1738-1822) was born in Hanover, Germany, but moved to England where he at first worked as a professional musician. His interest in astronomy led him to design and build his own telescopes.

MILESTONE

Herschel became famous for his discovery of the planet Uranus in 1781. Today he is remembered as one of the greatest astronomical observers. By studying the Milky Way over many years, he was able to make the first reasonably accurate estimate of its size and shape.

JOSEPH VON FRAUNHOFER (1787-1826) was an orphan who eventually became the director of a scientific institute in Germany. He was a trained optical worker who made some of the world's highest-quality telescope lenses.

MILESTONE

Fraunhofer identified and studied the dark absorption lines (now called Fraunhofer lines) in the solar spectrum. These lines enable scientists to tell which chemical elements are present in a source of light.

NEPTUNE (FIRST LOCATED IN 1846) The position of a new planet in the solar system was predicted mathematically. But its existence could not be confirmed until it had been observed.

MILESTONE

The "discovery" of Neptune was made possible by astronomers' increased understanding of the universe. Following the work of Newton and Halley, they were able to make increasingly accurate predictions about the behavior of objects in space.

WILLIAM HUGGINS (1824-1910) was an English astronomer who had his own private observatory in London. He was a pioneer of the technique of stellar spectroscopy (analysing the spectra produced by starlight).

MILESTONE

Huggins studied the light from many different stars. As a result of his work, he was able to show that stars are made of the same chemical elements that are found on Earth. He also showed that some nebulae are composed of gas.

GIOVANNI SCHIAPARELLI (1835-1910) was an Italian astronomer who became director of the Brera Observatory at Turin. He made headlines in 1877, when he claimed to be able to see a network of canals on Mars.

MILESTONE
Schiaparelli's most famous discovery was mistaken, but it did focus popular interest and attention on astronomy. He also established the link between comets and meteor showers.

EJNAR HERTZSPRUNG (1873-1967) and HENRY RUSSELL (1877-1957) were two scientists who, working independently, came to the same conclusions about the color and temperature of stars.

MILESTONE
The Hertzsprung-Russell (HR) diagram shows the relationship between surface temperature and color. Astronomers can identify the so-called "main sequence" of stellar development. Giant, supergiant, and dwarf stars are also located on the diagram.

ARTHUR EDDINGTON (1882-1945) was born in the north of England and became Professor of Astronomy at Cambridge. He was interested in the origin of stars, and he wrote science books for a general audience.

MILESTONE
Eddington was able to describe the structure of a star. He also explained how a star stays in one piece – balanced by the forces of gravity (pulling in), and gas pressure and radiation pressure (pushing out).

HARLOW SHAPLEY (1885-1972) was an American astronomer who became director of Harvard College Observatory. He used various stars as markers to study the distance and distribution of star clusters.

MILESTONE
Shapley was able to give the first accurate estimate of the size and shape of the Milky Way galaxy. He also showed that the Sun is located a very long way from the center of the galaxy.

CECILIA PAYNE-GAPOSCHKIN (1900-79) was born in England, but spent most of her working life at Harvard Observatory in the US. She is thought by many people to have been the greatest ever woman astronomer.

MILESTONE
By analysing the spectra of many different stars, Payne-Gaposchkin was able to show that all stars in the main sequence of development (the Sun for example) are composed almost entirely of the chemical elements hydrogen and helium.

EDWIN HUBBLE (1889-1953) was an American who began his working life as a lawyer before becoming a professional astronomer. He showed that the Andromeda spiral was definitely not part of the Milky Way galaxy.

MILESTONE
By showing that some objects are located outside the Milky Way, Hubble proved the existence of other galaxies. He also discovered that the universe appears to be constantly expanding.

GEORGES LEMAÎTRE (1894-1966) was a Belgian mathematician who worked in Britain and the US. His work had an important influence on the way that astronomers think about the universe.

MILESTONE
Lemaître proposed and developed the Big Bang theory about the origin of the universe. According to this theory, all matter and energy were created simultaneously by a huge explosion. This theory explains why many galaxies appear to be speeding away from us.

KARL JANSKY (1905-49) was an American radio engineer. While trying to solve the problem of static and interference with radio broadcasts, he discovered radio waves coming from the Milky Way.

MILESTONE
Without realizing it, Jansky discovered the basic techniques of radio astronomy. As a result of his work, astronomers have been able to to gather information from other parts of the electromagnetic spectrum, and not just from visible light.

FRED HOYLE (1915-2001) was a British astronomer who began his career as a mathematician. He became famous for his theory that life on Earth was the result of infection by bacteria from space carried by comets.

MILESTONE
Hoyle's most important work concerned the basic nuclear reactions at work deep inside stars. He explained the processes by which stars convert hydrogen into helium and other heavier elements.

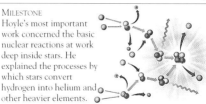

FRED WHIPPLE (b. 1906) was appointed professor of astronomy at Harvard in 1945, and became director of the Smithsonian Astrophysical Observatory in 1955. He is best known for his studies of comets and the solar system.

MILESTONE
His theory that comets are "dirty snowballs" has recently been proved correct by space probes such as Giotto. It now seems likely that comets are "leftovers" from the formation of the solar system.

ARNO PENZIAS (b. 1933) AND ROBERT WILSON (b. 1936) are American scientists. In 1978 they received the Nobel prize for physics for discovering the background radio energy of the universe – energy that is left over from the Big Bang.

MILESTONE
This radio energy ("the microwave background") gives the universe an average temperature about 5°F (3°C) above absolute zero. Many people believe that its discovery confirmed the Big Bang theory.

SUPERNOVA 1987A
The observation of a bright supernova during 1987 gave astronomers their first opportunity to study a supernova event with modern telescopes and other equipment.

MILESTONE
Analysis of the energy and particles produced by the event confirmed the theory that all chemical elements heavier than iron are made by very high-temperature nuclear reactions during supernova explosions.

SPACE MISSIONS I

THE SPACE AGE began in 1957 with the launch of the first satellite. Four years later Yuri Gagarin became the world's first astronaut. The next 20 years saw a surge of interest in space exploration.

FIRST SPACE VEHICLE
A model of Vostok I, the craft in which Yuri Gagarin made his historic first orbit of the Earth on April 12, 1961.

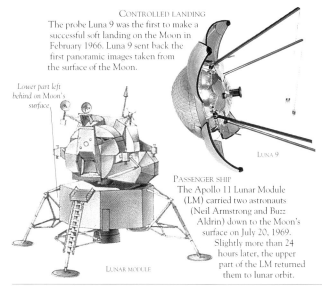

CONTROLLED LANDING
The probe Luna 9 was the first to make a successful soft landing on the Moon in February 1966. Luna 9 sent back the first panoramic images taken from the surface of the Moon.

Lower part left behind on Moon's surface

LUNA 9

PASSENGER SHIP
The Apollo 11 Lunar Module (LM) carried two astronauts (Neil Armstrong and Buzz Aldrin) down to the Moon's surface on July 20, 1969. Slightly more than 24 hours later, the upper part of the LM returned them to lunar orbit.

LUNAR MODULE

ROBOT MOON ROVER

Two Lunokhod robot vehicles were sent to the Moon in the early 1970s. Equipped with television cameras that enabled them to be driven from a control room on Earth, the two vehicles traveled a total of 29.5 miles (47.5 km) across the Moon.

Television camera

LUNOKHOD I

SCIENTIFIC PLATFORM

Launched in 1973, the Skylab orbiting laboratory and observatory gave astronauts the opportunity to work in space for weeks at a time. Skylab also enabled scientists to study the workings of Earth's atmosphere and climate systems from the viewpoint of space.

Apollo Telescope Mount

SKYLAB

MESSAGE TO THE STARS

The two Pioneer probes each carry a gold-covered plaque that shows a visual representation of human beings, as well as simple directions for locating the solar system and planet Earth.

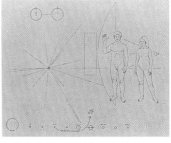

SPACE MISSIONS II

WORKING IN ORBIT became much easier with the introduction of the Space Shuttle in 1981. Probes have now visited all but one of the outer planets, and further exploration is planned.

The Shuttle has a mechanical arm which can be used to launch or retrieve satellites.

The external fuel tank breaks away at a height of 70 miles (110 km)

The booster rockets operate for about two minutes and are jettisoned at a height of 28 miles (45 km).

The Shuttle can lift off with eight crew and up to 32 tons (29 tonnes) of cargo.

INCREASING COMMUNICATIONS

The communications satellite Intelsat was launched by astronauts on the 49th Space Shuttle mission in May 1992. Improved communications is just one of the benefits of space technology now enjoyed by the general public.

ENDURANCE RECORD
Russian astronauts (cosmonauts) have
spent increasingly long periods of time
in space. The present record of 437
consecutive days was achieved aboard
the space station Mir during 1994-95.
The picture shows a cosmonaut on the
rigorous exercise program devised to
keep the crew in shape during long
periods of weightlessness. Mir burned up
when it reentered Earth's atmosphere in
2001, after 18 years in orbit.

ROSETTA PROBE

COMET-CHASER
The Rosetta orbiter/lander
(right) will attempt to
rendezvous with a comet.
The lander will detach
from the orbiter and
descend to the comet's nucleus.
Having anchored itself to the surface, it will
transmit data to the orbiter, for relaying back
to Earth. Scientists hope that Rosetta will
shed light on how comets form.

CASSINI-HUYGENS PROBE
Launched in 1997, Cassini
will reach Saturn in 2004
and then spend four years
studying the planet and its
moons. On arrival, Cassini
will release the mini-probe
Huygens, which will touch
down on Titan, the largest
of Saturn's many moons.

Glossary

ABSORPTION LINES
Thin dark lines across a spectrum which indicate the presence of chemical elements in the light source.

ACCRETION DISK
A structure formed by material spiraling around a star or a black hole.

ASTEROID
A lump of rock orbiting the Sun. Most asteroids are found in a narrow belt situated between Mars and Jupiter.

ASTRONAUT
Someone who travels through space.

ASTRONOMY
The scientific study of objects in space.

ATMOSPHERE
Layer of gases surrounding a planet, moon, or star.

AXIS (OF SPIN)
An imaginary line through a rotating object, around which the object rotates.

BIG BANG
The explosion that created the universe about 15 billion years ago.

BLACK HOLE
An infinitely dense object formed initially by the collapse of a massive star. The gravity of a black hole is so strong that not even light can escape from it.

CELESTIAL EQUATOR
A projection of Earth's equator out into space, used as a baseline for measuring the positions of stars.

CELESTIAL POLE
Projection of Earth's north or south pole into space, for use as a reference point.

CELESTIAL SPHERE
The appearance of the stars from Earth – as though they were set into a black sphere around the planet.

CHROMOSPHERE
The Sun's inner atmosphere.

CLUSTER
A grouping of stars or galaxies held by gravity.

COMET
An object composed of snow and dust that orbits the Sun. If a comet approaches the Sun it forms a tail of gas and dust particles.

CONSTELLATION
A grouping of bright stars seen in Earth's sky. In most cases the grouping is a trick of perspective and the stars are a long way apart.

CO-ORBITAL
Sharing an orbital path with another object.

CORE
The central region of a planet, star, or galaxy.

CORONA
The Sun's outer atmosphere.

CRATER
Circular depression in the surface of a planet or a moon caused by a meteorite impact.

CRUST
The surface layer of a rock planet or moon.

ECLIPSE
The effect produced when one object in

space enters the shadow of another and becomes darkened or obscured.

ECLIPTIC
The Sun's apparent path around the celestial sphere during a year.

ELECTROMAGNETIC SPECTRUM
The spectrum of radiated energy which includes: gamma rays, X-rays, ultraviolet rays, visible light, infrared radiation, microwaves, and radio and television signals.

ESCAPE VELOCITY
The speed needed to overcome the gravitational pull of a celestial body.

FLYBY
The path of a space probe that passes a moon or a planet without going into orbit around it.

GALAXY
A large grouping of stars held together by gravity. Galaxies can be spiral, elliptical (oval), or irregular in shape.

GRAVITY
An attractive force that is a property of mass.

GREENHOUSE EFFECT
Increased heating of a planetary atmosphere due to an excess of carbon dioxide.

HELIOSPHERE
The volume of space swept by charged particles from the Sun.

HEMISPHERE
One half of a sphere. The term is usually applied to regions north or south of an equator.

LIGHT-YEAR (LY)
The distance traveled by light in one year – used to measure distances between stars and galaxies.

LOCAL ARM
Name often given to the Orion arm – the spiral arm of the Milky Way galaxy in which the Sun is located.

LOCAL GROUP
The cluster of galaxies of which the Milky Way galaxy is a member.

LUMINOSITY
The amount of light energy produced by a light source.

MAGNETIC FIELD
The region around a magnetic source within which the magnetic force operates.

MAGNETOSPHERE
The volume of space influenced by a planet's magnetic field.

MAGNITUDE
The brightness of a star or galaxy. Apparent magnitude is the brightness as actually seen from Earth. Absolute magnitude is the brightness if seen from a standard distance of about 32.5 light-years.

MAIN SEQUENCE
A stage in the life cycle of stars during which they produce energy through the conversion of hydrogen to helium.

MANTLE
The molten layer beneath the crust of a rock planet.

MASS
The amount of matter in an object. The Sun's mass (1 solar mass) is used as a standard for measuring the mass of stars and galaxies.

MATTER
Anything that occupies space. There are three states of matter – gas, liquid, and solid.

MESSIER CATALOG
A list of bright clusters, galaxies, and nebulae compiled in 1781.

METEOR
A streak of light in the sky caused by a rock or dust particle from space burning up because of atmospheric friction.

METEORITE
A piece of rock or metal from space that impacts on the surface of a planet or moon.

METEOROID
A fragment of rock or metal in space.

MILKY WAY
The spiral galaxy which contains billions of stars including the Sun.

MINOR PLANETS
Asteroids

MOON
A natural satellite of a planet. Earth's moon is the Moon.

NEBULA
A cloud of gas and dust in space. Some nebulae glow, others are dark.

NEUTRON STAR
A star that has collapsed into a super-dense form of matter. Some neutron stars are seen as pulsars.

NEW GENERAL CATALOG
A list of clusters, galaxies, and nebulae first published in 1888.

NUCLEAR FUSION
The power source of stars. A reaction in which atoms fuse together giving off large amounts of energy.

NUCLEUS
The central part of an atom, comet, or galaxy.

OBSERVATORY
A building that contains an astronomical telescope.

ORBIT
The path of one object in space around another.

ORBITAL PERIOD
The time taken for an object to make one complete orbit.

ORBITAL VELOCITY
The velocity required to maintain an orbit.

PARALLAX METHOD
A way of calculating the distance to stars by measuring the apparent shift in their position.

PENUMBRA
The outer part of the shadow cast during an eclipse. Also, the outer

and warmer part of a sunspot.

PERIODIC COMET
A comet that comes close to the Sun at regular intervals.

PHOTOSPHERE
The Sun's visible surface.

PLANET
A spherical object, composed of rock or liquefied gas, that orbits around a star.

PRESSURE
The force acting on a given area of surface.

PROMINENCE
A jet of gas arising from the Sun's surface.

PROTON-PROTON CHAIN
The main type of fusion reaction inside stars whereby hydrogen is converted into helium.

PROTOSTAR
A very young star that has not begun to shine.

PULSAR
A rapidly rotating neutron star that gives off beams of energy.

QUASAR
A very bright and distant object believed to be the core of a very young galaxy.

RADAR-MAPPING
A technique for producing relief maps from radar signals.

RADIANT
The point in the sky from which a meteor shower appears to come.

RADIATION
Forms of energy able to travel across space.

RED GIANT
A stage in the life cycle of many stars when they increase in size and begin the conversion of helium to carbon.

RED SHIFT
A shift towards the red end of the spectrum seen in light from sources that are moving away from the Earth.

ROTATION PERIOD
The time taken for an object to make one complete axial rotation.

SATELLITE
An object orbiting around a planet. There are natural satellites (moons), and artificial satellites put in orbit by human beings.

SOLAR PANELS
Electronic devices that produce electricity when placed in sunlight.

SOLAR SYSTEM
The Sun, and all the planets, moons, asteroids, and comets that orbit around it.

SOLAR WIND
A stream of electrically charged particles given off by the Sun.

SPACE
The volume between objects in the universe.

SPECTROHELIOSCOPE
A special telescope for studying the Sun.

SPECTRUM
Display of the different wavelengths or frequencies that make up radiated energy.

STAR
A large spinning ball of very hot gas that generates energy by nuclear fusion.

SUNSPOTS
Dark, irregular patches that are visible on the Sun's surface.

SUPERCLUSTER
A huge cluster that is itself made up of clusters of galaxies.

SUPERNOVA
The explosion of a large star, which may briefly produce more light than an entire galaxy.

TELESCOPE
A device for seeing at a distance. Optical telescopes use mirrors and lenses. Radio telescopes use metal dishes to "see" radio signals. Other telescopes are sensitive to other forms of energy.

UMBRA
The inner part of the shadow cast during a solar or lunar eclipse. Also, the inner and cooler part of a sunspot.

UNIVERSE
Everything that exists.

VACUUM
Space empty of matter.

WAVELENGTH
A characteristic feature of radiant energy.

WEIGHTLESSNESS
Condition of apparent zero gravity experienced by space travelers.

WHITE DWARF
The collapsed core of a Sun-sized star.

ZODIAC
The 12 constellations through which the Sun appears to travel during one year.

Index

Acknowledgments

Dorling Kindersley would like to thank:
Caroline Potts for sympathetic photo-librarianship, Robert Graham, Ray Rogers and Connie Mersel for cheerful assistance, Hilary Bird for the index, and Dr. David W. Hughes of Sheffield University for his much appreciated professional advice.

Illustrations by:
Julian Baum, Rick Blakely, Luciano Corbella, Richard Draper, Mike Grey, Jeremy Gower, John Hutchinson, Andrew Macdonald, J. Marffy, Daniel J. Pyne, Pete Serjeant, Guy Smith, Taurus Graphics, Raymond Turvey, François Vincent, Richard Ward, Brian Watson, John Woodcock

Picture credits: t = top b = bottom
c = center l = left r = right
Anglo Australian Telescope Board/D. Malin: 37tr, 42/43. Rob Beighton 83cl. The Bodleian Library, University of Oxford: 142bl. ESO/Meylan: 126tr, 137tl. European Space Agency: 131c, 131bl, 151cr, 151bl. European Southern Observatory: 129cl. Mary Evans Picture Library: 142cl, 143tr, 143crb, 143 br, 144tl. FLPA: 46tr; Genesis Space Photo Library 10/11, 127t. Harvard University Archives: 146t. Image Select/Ann Ronan: 144b, 145t. IPAC: 24tr. JPL courtesy of NOAO: 112tl. Lund Observatory: 25tl. Mansell Collection: 143rct, 144tc. NASA: 27tl, 84tr, 90cl, 92tr, 98cl, 104tr, 106cl, 130tr, 130b, 136tr, 139t; CXC/SAO 121br, 131t; James Bell (Cornell Univ.), Michael Wolff, (Space Science Inst.) and the Hubble Heritage Team (STScI/AURA) 88tr; JPL

16bl, 21tr, 28/29, 30tr, 32tr, 54tr, 60/61, 66tr, 68bl, 70/71, 73tl, 76tr, 77tr, 79tl, 80tl, 81tl, 85tl, 89tr, 93tr, 96tr, 97tr, 100tr, 101bl, 105tr, 108tr, 118/119, 127b, 133cl, 134tr, 138tr, 140/141, 144clb, 147cb, 148/149, 149cl, 150cr; JPL/North Western University 72ti, JPL/University of Arizona 92tr; JPL/University of Arizona/Los Alamos National Laboratories 126b; Palomar Obs 121cl; W M Keck Obs 121tr. NOAO/AURA/NSF: Bill Schoening, Vanessa Harvey/REU program 20tl. Novosti: 151tl. Science Photo Library: Alex Bariel 122tr; Dr Jeremy Burgess 142tl; European Southern Observatory 13tr; European Space Agency 113br, 113cl; Fred Espenak 45t; François Gohier 124tr; Max Planck Institut fur Radioastronomy 124bl, 146b; David Mclean 114tr; NASA 116tr, 127cl, 138br, 139b; NOAO 18/19; Pekka Parviainen 47tl; Roger Ressmeyer, Starlight 44tr; Royal Observatory Edinburgh/Anglo-Australian Telescope Board 22tr, 26bl, 50tr, 110/111; Royal Greenwich Observatory 125cl; John Sanford 48tr, 115br; Dr. Seth Shostak 125tl; Starsem 132tr. Starland Picture Library/ESO 35tl. UPI/Bettman 146cr.

Every effort has been made to trace the copyright holders and we apologise in advance for any unintentional omissions. We would be pleased to insert the appropriate acknowledgment in any subsequent edition of this publication.

All other images © Dorling Kindersley
For further information see:
www.dkimages.com